η

94

BIOGRAPHY **Gerassi, John.,** 1931–
    CASTRO   Fidel Castro; a biography.   Doubleday ₍c1973₎   137p.
                3.95

            The story of the leader of Cuba's 1959 revolution and of
        the revolution itself, its historical background, its achieve-
        ments and consequences.

                                                    12617

                    1. Castro, Fidel, 1927-   2. Cuba—History.
                                                                    D73

        LJ Cards, c1973

9

FIDEL CASTRO

A Biography

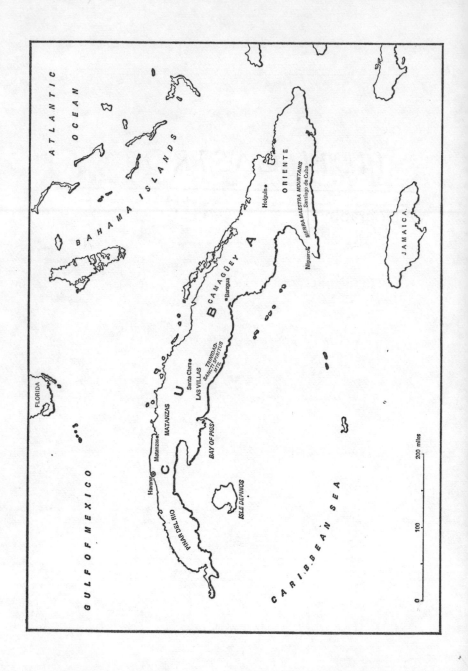

ATLANTIC OCEAN

BAHAMA ISLANDS

JAMAICA

GULF OF MEXICO

FLORIDA

CUBA

PINAR DEL RIO

MATANZAS

Havana

Matanzas

Santa Clara

LAS VILLAS

TRINIDAD-
SANCTI SPIRITUS
MTS.

BAY OF PIGS

ISLE DE PINOS

CAMAGÜEY

Baragua

Holguín

ORIENTE

SIERRA MAESTRA MOUNTAINS
Santiago de Cuba

Niquero

CARIBBEAN SEA

0   100   200 miles

FIDEL CASTRO

A Biography

By John Gerassi

DOUBLEDAY & COMPANY, INC.
GARDEN CITY, NEW YORK   1973

ISBN: 0-385-02791-5 Trade
       0-385-04076-8 Prebound
Library of Congress Catalog Card Number 70–180076
Copyright © 1973 by John Gerassi
All Rights Reserved
Printed in the United States of America
First Edition

Jenny James García did the research. She's the one who deserves the credit.

1

"I'm a professional revolutionary," Fidel Castro once said to a French writer.

"What does that mean?" asked the writer.

"It means," replied Fidel, poking the forefinger of his right hand into the writer's belly so as to emphasize the point, "that I can't stand injustice."

Yet Fidel was not personally afflicted by injustices. He was not born poor. He liked his mother and was liked by her. He got along well enough with his brothers and sisters. He had good teachers at school, and they encouraged him in his studies. And even as a young boy he was free to roam his father's plantation during summer vacations almost at will. Where, then, did his burning hatred of injustice come from?

From Cuba itself. The whole country was an island of injustice. Fidel could see it in school. He felt it when wandering the lush hills of his native Oriente Province. He rebelled against it even when his father's peons accepted it. Injustice was impossible to avoid in those days, for Cuba was a country of hair-raising contrasts: a few, very few, rich people, mostly foreigners, and six million poor.

The poor lived in *bohios*, stark houses with thatched roofs, improvised walls of bark from palm trees, and dirt floors. They had no toilets, no water, no electricity. They could not afford to send their children to school, and the few schools around were for the children of the rich anyway. Children of the poor rarely ate meat or green vegetables, only cheap foods: the fried bananas, sweet potatoes, and yucca, which made their stomachs swell like balloons. They had no chance of getting the vitamins needed to fight off deadly germs or infections.

The worst of these infections came from tiny green-gray worms which infested the untilled lands where the poor kids played. As their parents could not afford to buy them shoes, they went barefoot, and the worms worked their way into the soles of their naked feet, up into the stomach and grew to the size of lead pencils; many of the children died.

Only during the *zafra*, the sugar harvest, did it seem as if people were happy. It was then that hundreds of thousands of peasants, swinging the long, flat, sharp knife known as the *machete*, cut down millions of tons of sugar-cane stalks. Sugar stalks grow ten feet tall and are three times as fat and tough as cornstalks. It takes a lot of strength and energy to cut them down, trim off the leaves, and pile them up into the carts which haul them off to the mills. So during the zafra, rural families had to buy meat and rice to build up their men, who had to work twelve and often fourteen hours every day. The men also had to buy long-sleeve shirts, shoes, and gloves to protect their skin from the white dust of the cane, which can cause terrible rashes. Thus, no worker could save any money during the zafra.

Still, it was then that rural towns came alive. Traveling salesmen, peddling imported food and clothing, crowded second-class hotels and animated local cafes. Lights appeared in the countryside as families suddenly had a few pennies to buy kerosene for their lamps. But then, after two months or so, the zafra would end. The sugar plantation owners started cutting down their costs. Workers began to beg for steady jobs at lower pay. Storekeepers reduced their stock. The traveling salesmen returned to Havana. The lights in the bohios flickered out. The cane cutter stopped drinking coffee; instead he made his own cane juice in a crude wooden hand press installed in his doorway. Many families moved on, looking for work elsewhere. There was none to be found. Then came the rains and with them the malaria mosquito. But by then there was no money left for doctors or medicine.

The sugar plantation owners, of course, had lots of money. Each year, after they sold their sugar abroad, they used some of their profits to stake out more land. Huge tracts of good mahogany and cedar timbers were cut down. Once the lumber was moved, the area was set ablaze to clear it com-

3

pletely, and the sugar was planted. By the end of the Second World War, half of the whole island was given to sugar. That meant almost nothing else could be raised or planted. The result was that a country which was rich agriculturally could not feed itself. Even staples—rice, wheat, corn—had to be imported, at higher and higher prices. The poor got poorer and poorer, and ate worse and worse.

How could it all happen that way?

Cuba, the pearl of the Antilles, one of the most beautiful islands in the world, was one of the first discovered by the Spaniards—almost five centuries ago. It was immediately exploited for the benefit of the Spanish crown. When the local Indians rebelled, they were slaughtered and replaced by destitute immigrants from the poor sections of Spain, mainly northeastern Galicia. What the Spanish poor wouldn't do, imported African slaves did—at the point of a gun.

As soon as the United States had consolidated its western territory, it too coveted Cuba. Lying only ninety miles southeast of Florida, Cuba was so much of a temptation to greedy Americans that they abandoned all semblance of fair play when talking about it. Thus one senator said point-blank in 1858: "It is our destiny to have Cuba and it is folly to debate the question. It naturally belongs to the American continent." John L. O'Sullivan, editor of the most important journal of the times, the New York *Morning News*, had already made clear America's interest. He had said in 1845: "Our manifest destiny is to occupy and to possess the whole continent." Almost every American politician was anxious to take over Cuba, and almost every big-time American businessman was thirsting to exploit its riches. No one much cared what the Cubans wanted.

What they wanted, however, was independence. In 1868, they finally rebelled against Spain. The Cuban revolutionaries had only machetes and hunting muskets. The Spaniards had modern weapons including cannons and the world's second largest navy. (England, which had the biggest, remained neutral.)

What's more, the Spanish forces could rely on the big landowners for financial aid, and they used terror and torture to force ordinary Cubans to help them. Nevertheless, the war lasted ten years. Some eighty thousand Spanish soldiers died during that time, and a large part of the Cuban countryside was laid waste. Spanish fortunes had been destroyed and the country was ruined.

It was easy, then, for American businessmen to pick up the pieces. Between 1880 and 1890, they came in droves. They bought up many of the sugar plantations and took over most of the mines. Naturally, neither these tycoons nor the United States Government were very happy about the taxes going to Spain. So both wanted the Cubans to rebel again against Spain. America gave asylum to Cuban patriots, offered them money, and promised to "leave the government and control of the island to its people" if the rebellion was successful.

José Martí, Cuba's George Washington, did not believe these promises. He had lived too long in America and knew that rich businessmen will say anything in order to get what they want, but once they get it never keep their promises—if they can help it. So, Martí tried to stir his compatriots to rebel against Spain on their own.

They did, in 1895. Within three years it was clear that they would win. But if they did, American tycoons said, Cuba would not be American. It would be free to be what its people wanted. That, insisted these tycoons, must not happen. "Cuba is too rich an island," they said, "for it not to belong to us." And so they pushed the United States Government to do something about it.

What the United States did was declare war on Spain. It did so under the pretext that it was the Spaniards who were responsible for the sinking of the U.S. battleship *Maine* when it was berthed in the harbor of Havana. A lot of American sailors died in that explosion, and it was easy for the American press to convince the American public that Spain ought to be punished for the loss of these American lives. Of course, Washington, the American tycoons, and the owners of the newspapers knew that Spain had nothing to do with the *Maine* disaster. The mines had, in fact, been planted on the battleship by

American agents, precisely to give America an excuse to go to war against Spain.

But it worked. The American people demanded vengeance and the U.S. Marines invaded Cuba. The war lasted less than four months. Spain was defeated. And America occupied not only Cuba but two other island countries then under Spanish rule: Puerto Rico and the Philippines. (For the next fifty years, the people of the Philippines rebelled against America, demanding independence. But like Cuba, the Philippines was very rich and American businessmen owned most of the industry. So each time the Filipinos rebelled, America called them bandits and massacred them. After the Second World War, the Philippines finally became independent. But its government was put in by the U.S. Army and to this day it is controlled by Washington.)

For the people of Puerto Rico, fate has been more tragic. The island was immediately "Americanized." Its industry was welded to American industry. Its money, its judges, its draft laws became American. Puerto Rico decayed into a complete American colony. It still is—despite the fact that the United Nations has asked Washington to give Puerto Rico its independence.

In Cuba, meanwhile, colonization was not so simple. After all, too many Cubans had fought for independence to accept American rule. No sooner had the Spanish Army left Cuba than Cuban patriots started shouting, "Yankee, go home." It soon became clear to Washington that if the U.S. Marines stayed and turned Cuba into another American colony, Cubans would rebel again and again. And so an ingenious plot was devised in Washington. It was called the Platt Amendment, in infamous honor of the senator who thought it up.

The Platt Amendment was a series of provisions which Cubans had to add to their "independent" constitution before the U.S. Army of Occupation would leave the island. Cubans knew the provisions were outrageous, but America was too strong. And, after years of struggle, Cubans were too confused and too tired to fully understand what would happen. Their great revolutionary leader José Martí had been shot and killed during the fighting, and no one else seemed capable of rallying all the people. So Cubans accepted the Platt Amendment and put it into their constitution.

The Platt Amendment turned Cuba into a colony of the United States without the use of U.S. Marines. Article III, for example, gave the United States the right to take over Cuba each time it—the United States—thought that a particular Cuban government, no matter how popular with Cubans, was not giving enough protection to its inhabitants' "life, property and individual liberty." What that meant was that any time an American businessman who was exploiting his workers too much was threatened with legal action, U.S. Marines could take over the island.

Article IV of the Platt Amendment gave America the right to maintain bases on Cuban soil and to station U.S. troops there for immediate action in Cuba should there be unrest among the Cuban people. Soon every Cuban understood that those troops would barge right in if any American businessman yelled for help. The result was that these same businessmen bought up the country, controlled its trade, financed its political parties, and from behind the scenes even trained and commanded its army. American troops left Cuba (except for the bases) in 1902, but Cuba was as much a colony as Puerto Rico. Things got so bad that in most Cuban schools it was all right to talk during the playing of the Cuban national anthem so long as each child stood rigidly at attention during "The Star Spangled Banner."

Cubans could do little about such a situation. They were too weak to rebel, so, for the next few decades, they simply gave up. Meanwhile, one corrupt government after another ruled the country with American help. Havana became a port of luxury—for the rich and the American tourist. Fancy hotels were built along the seashore. Gambling casinos, run by American gangsters, flourished. Prostitution, drugs, vice of every kind were protected by the police—because that's what the tourists wanted.

Franklin D. Roosevelt got rid of the Platt Amendment after he was elected President of the United States. But, by then, it was too late; every Cuban official was tied to American interests. Still, as bad as it was, sometimes a Cuban ruler overdid it. General Gerardo Machado, for example, was so vicious that he was nicknamed "the butcher." In 1933, led by Havana University students, the Cuban people rebelled against him and forced him to flee the country. They then gave the presidency to a respected intellectual, Dr. Ramón Grau San Martín. He was less corrupt than the others. He tried to rule democratically. He even instituted some reforms. But they angered American businessmen. So the United States refused to accept his government. The result was that old Dr. Grau was overthrown by the Cuban Army, led by Fulgencio Batista. Naturally, America recognized Batista's regime.

To satisfy America's demand for a "good image," Batista allowed some semblance of democracy. He put in a figurehead as president and ruled from behind. Not all political parties were banned and congressional elections did take place. Though his secret police were brutal and bloody, Batista thought he was popular. The American public relation agents working for him even convinced him he could win a presidential election. Finally, in 1952, he decided to run for President—and let other candidates run against him.

Immediately, the opposition mushroomed. It became clear he would lose. So with the aid of the Army he seized control of the country. The farce of democracy was over: Batista was now out in the open again as the vicious dictator he really was.

Nor did Batista have to hide the identity of his real bosses any more. American businesses took over 90 per cent of Cuba's utilities, cattle ranches and, with the aid of British capital, all of Cuba's oil companies. "The United States was so overwhelmingly influential in Cuba," said United States Ambassador to Cuba, E. T. Smith, "that the American Ambassador was the second most important man in Cuba, sometimes even more important than the President of Cuba." The way the Cubans put it was: "Poor Cuba, so far from God, so near the United States."

And, of course, the Cuban people got poorer. Not just in the countryside where such American enterprises as the United Fruit Company and Standard Fruit Company continued to expand their sugar holdings to the detriment of the island's food supply, but in fancy Havana as well.

True, if you were a rich Cuban you lived well, just like the American company executives. You were addicted to American sports. You read such American funnies as *Li'l Abner* and *Dick Tracy*. You went to gaudy night clubs and sat next to American stars and celebrities. The beach you swam at was raked and cleaned every day by young blacks who were not allowed to swim there themselves. Your home in the new Vedado district was a sprawling tiled villa kept spanking clean by a squad of uniformed maids.

Chances are you didn't even see how the others lived—the maids' parents or her children—in their *solares,* one-room shacks lining the alleys of old Havana. A dozen people to one room. No water. No sanitation—except for one outside toilet for each *solar* of two hundred or more people. And everywhere Batista's police, keeping tabs, rooting out gripers, killing off potential troublemakers.

But it wasn't only the poor who hated Batista. The country's university students were also against him. Young and idealistic, aware of their country's unhappy history, the students wanted freedom to think, to talk, to write, to work, to build Cuba into a proud solvent land. They wanted real independence, not the foreign brand. They wanted to eliminate poverty, ignorance, racism. And so they tried to mold an opposition to Batista.

For this they were hunted down, beaten, and killed by Batista's police. Headed by a man called Ventura, Batista's police never hesitated to kill or torture the innocent in the hope of catching a dissenter. Here's just one case, told by a young woman who today acts as an interpreter for foreign visitors:

"My brother, my only brother, was a wonderful young man. Everybody predicted a brilliant career for him. He was tall, graceful, one of the city's handsomest men. One night he came to my apartment to stay over, as he often did. Near dawn I heard voices in the living room, and throwing on my robe, I ran out. There were Ventura's men—and Ventura —holding my brother, and they were about to take him out of the door. I rushed forward and asked Ventura why. Oh, I knew Ventura, that darling of

society! So polite, the soul of grace! Always dressed
à la mode in his latest cut, white silk suit. He smiled,
and said, 'Don't worry, my dear, we just are check-
ing a few things, everything will be all right.'

"My heart sank for I knew Ventura's reputation;
he would often attend a soiree and when he got a
telephone call, he would ask everybody's pardon saying duty calls, and he would leave. We knew why.
They had caught a revolutionary or suspect. We
heard how he carried a small, pearl-handled re-
volver in his inside pocket. And we knew that he
would use other weapons just to get them to 'talk.'
When he took my brother, I almost died."

She dressed quickly, rushed to the dreaded Barracks No. 3 where "talking" took place. The police
denied knowing anything. For three days she went
from one police barracks to another.

"I called all our family's friends. Many were in
high places. One told me that they suspected my
brother of hiding guns for the revolutionaries. When
I finally caught up with my brother, they told me I
could take care of him. When they let me see him,
he was unrecognizable. His eyes were swollen closed
and black; his face was a mass of blood; he lay
moaning and he did not recognize me. I got an am-
bulance and a doctor and brought him home. I
nursed him for weeks while he lay in delirium and
failed to recognize me. When he finally regained
his mind, he was a broken man. He never smiled. He
showed no emotion. He talked in a flat, dull voice,

13

this young brother of mine who was always laughing."

Every student under Batista risked such an outcome. Whether they came from rich families or poor, Batista could not trust students because he could not trust anyone who thought for himself, anyone who had not been corrupted. One such student under Batista was Fidel Castro Ruz.

2

Fidel was born on August 13, 1926, on his father's ranch at Mayarí, a small town in Oriente Province. His father, Angel Castro, was a Spaniard from Galicia. He had come to Cuba in 1898 as a soldier—to fight the Cuban rebels. After Spain's defeat, he had stayed on and went to work for the Nipe Bay Company, a United Fruit subsidiary, as a manual laborer. Seven years and probably a lot of stealing later, he bought a small plantation at Mayarí. In the years that followed, a struggle developed between two groups of landowners and their peons. Angel was on the side of the winners and so expanded his acreage from the confiscated land of the losers.

Angel's first wife, a schoolteacher, died young, and Angel soon married Lina Ruz, who had also come from Spain and had been his servant. They had five children: Ramón, Fidel, Raúl, Emma, and Juanna. As the oldest, Ramón was looked after closely by his father; it was clear that Angel expected Ramón to take over the plantation, and it wasn't long before

Ramón, not without some trepidation, accepted that future. But Fidel and Raúl had no such interest. As young kids, they roamed the nearby hills and explored the base of the local mountains, known as the Sierra Maestra.

In these wanderings, the boys discovered how ordinary Cubans lived. They met neighboring farmers who tried to make do on barren land, surviving in hovels with neither light nor plumbing. They understood the dangers of ignorance and the importance of learning.

But neither Angel nor his wife had had an education, and they saw no reason to send more than one child to school. That would be for Ramón, so he could learn to expand the business. But not for Fidel or Raúl.

One day, when Fidel was six, he walked into the comfortable living area of Angel's house and, facing his father squarely, said: "Papa, I want to go to school."

Angel looked up and smiled. Then he saw that Fidel, his eyes burning, was very serious.

"Listen, child," Angel shouted, getting up, "I didn't go to school, no reason you should."

Fidel remained motionless. He stared into his father's eyes. Then slowly but firmly he said, "I *shall* go to school, or else . . ." He stopped. Angel came up to him and prepared to slap his face. "Or else what?" he shouted menacingly.

Fidel stared unflinchingly, then calmly finished

his sentence. "Or else," he said, "I'll burn this whole place down to the ground."

Angel hesitated, turned away, mumbling, "We'll see." But he knew the boy meant it. And so both Fidel and Raúl went to school.

Tall, healthy, curious, Fidel did well, first at the Mayarí parish school, then at the Jesuit Colegio (grammar school) of Santiago, capital of Oriente Province. But soon he was in trouble. It all started one day at lunchtime. "Look," he said to his brother Raúl eating beside him, "see what they are serving the poor?" Raúl looked over at the next table. They had no meat on their plates. Fidel and Raúl had meat.

After lunch, Fidel went over to the nun in charge of the dining room. "Sister, why do we get meat and they don't?" he asked, pointing to the poor.

"Because, my child," she answered, "you come from homes where meat is always served. You are used to meat. They aren't. They don't expect it. They don't get it at home, why should they get it here . . ."

Fidel thought it over for a day. "It's not fair," he told Raúl. "They get the same teachers, they must wear the same uniforms, why shouldn't they eat the same?"

"What can we do about it?" asked Raúl.

"Organize a strike," answered Fidel.

And so they did. They convinced a few of the rich boys who ate meat that it wasn't fair, and they talked most of the poor boys into protesting. On the next Monday, both groups refused to eat anything or to move from their tables until everyone had been served the same food. The school authorities were very upset, and Fidel and Raúl were kicked out.

"Well," said Fidel much later, "that was my first defeat. There were many more. But it made me angry."

It also made him more sensitive to other injustices. One such injustice was the way his own father treated his peons. "He made them work long and hard, and paid them almost nothing," Fidel said. And so, when he was thirteen, Fidel tried to organize his father's sugar workers to strike against him. He talked and he talked until his father finally heard about it, gave him a lashing and shipped him off to a much stricter Jesuit school in Havana. "Angel," said Fidel, "was one of those who abuse the powers they wrench from the people with deceitful promises." But as his father's son he respected his wishes, and accepted the new school without rancor.

He worked hard, was an excellent swimmer and runner, and, already almost six feet tall, was a great asset on the basketball team. One of his schoolmates remembers him as "nervous, somber, driven by relentless pride. It was enough for some undertaking to be called impossible for him to throw himself into it." He finished high school with honors in 1945. Said the year book: "Fidel distinguished himself always in all subjects related to letters. His record was one of excellence; he was a true athlete, always defending with bravery and pride the flag of the school. He has known how to win the admiration and affection of all. He will make law his career and we do not doubt that he will fill with brilliant pages the book of his life. He has good timber and the actor in him will not be lacking."

And so, at nineteen, muscular, six feet tall and still growing, Fidel Castro entered Havana University. It is traditional in Latin America for students to be politically active. Fidel was no exception. In fact, with his stature, amazing speaking ability, and rebellious if not quarrelsome temperament, Fidel went into politics with both feet.

The son of a well-off family of landowners, Fidel was, nevertheless, not spoiled. The income he received from Angel was very small, just enough to get by without extras. But the gay life wasn't for him anyway. He was studious and serious. He quickly gained the respect of his fellow students and some solid followers as well. Havana University, he said, "was full of frustrated revolutionaries who had become caricatures. These caricatures were organized into rival gangs. Armed to the teeth, they claimed to be fighting for 'our liberation.' But, in fact, they killed each other off in order to get power. Power to be the only ones to sell duplicated copies of courses. Power to kidnap and ransom rich students. Power to control the illegal sale of diplomas and obtain the paying jobs in the Student Federation. In passing they terrorized the teaching staff."

Fidel could have been a natural for one of these armed groups. He was audacious. He knew how to handle firearms. He was very political but had no sound political training and could have been enticed by the fancy words of one of these groups. But Fidel never sought action or adventure for its own sake. He always had to be convinced of the goals—and that they were worthwhile.

So, Fidel remained an independent. He campaigned alone, or with a few equally independent followers, for better school government, for an end to corruption, for an end to the killing. To the leaders of the armed groups, therefore, he became a danger. One day, one of these leaders, a certain Mario Salabarria who headed a group with the phony name of the Revolutionary Socialist Movement, ordered Fidel's execution. His henchmen set up an ambush, near the small room where Fidel lived alone. But just before they opened fire on him with automatic weapons, Fidel sensed something. Running at top speed, he jumped over a car and dived into an embankment, as bullets whizzed over his head.

Fidel had escaped. To make sure he was not attacked again, he then joined a rival group but stayed independent of its actions. In a local newspaper, he denounced these armed groups as pseudo revolutionaries paid by the police. Nevertheless, *Hoy*, the

Communist newspaper, denounced Fidel as a gangster.

Fidel counterattacked by accusing the Law Students' Association, which was run by the Communists, of corruption. He had gotten himself elected its vice-president, and so he had access to a great deal of information. This now made him a target for Communist gunmen, and Fidel not only had to be constantly armed, but he also had to keep his home and movements secret. Eventually, his exposé convinced even the Communist Party, which did not approve of corruption by its members. The Party forced the Law Students' Association president to resign and supported Fidel when he stepped up to take the presidency.

Meanwhile, Fidel was learning fast. Not only about Cuban politics, but also about the situation all over the world. He grew to despise despots of all kinds and, in 1947, singled out one of the worst at that time: Rafael Trujillo, dictator of the nearby Dominican Republic. He joined a group of real revolutionaries who were training to launch an invasion of that island, in the hope of unleashing a move to overthrow Trujillo.

In 1947, Batista was still exercising power from his barracks headquarters, he was not yet President. That slot was temporarily occupied by Grau San Martín, and Batista let him handle his foreign affairs as he wished. Grau had no love for Trujillo. So he turned a blind eye on the preparations going on in Cayo Confites, on the Oriente shore across from the Dominican Republic.

But at the same time the foreign ministers of the whole American continent were meeting in Brazil to discuss mutual problems. At one of the sessions, the Dominican delegate got up and denounced Cuba for allowing an invasion of his country to be staged from Cuban soil. The Dominican had such accurate information and described so precisely what was going on in Cayo Confites that Grau felt obliged to put a stop to it. The trouble was that on the day Grau ordered the halt the yacht with the revolutionaries got under way. So the Cuban Navy was sent to intercept it.

Rather than face a trial, Fidel decided to make a run for it. Or, in this case, a swim. With two comrades, their Tommy guns slung around their necks, Fidel dived into the shark-infested Caribbean Sea and swam three miles to safety. "Just another of my many failures," Fidel said later, laughing. "Each one taught me something. Each one determined me more."

Back at law school, Fidel had an immediate new issue. Traditionally, black students were barred from the athletic teams. Fidel thought that was outrageous. He organized a committee to end racial discrimination at the university, gained massive support from his comrades, and won at least a small battle: discrimination in sports ended.

But, by then, an Anti-Colonialist and Anti-Imperialist Student Congress had been scheduled for Bogotá, the capital of Colombia. Fidel and his friend Rafael del Pino had been the main organizers of the Cuban section of the Congress. So they went to Bogotá.

Fidel wanted to push three main points: independence for Puerto Rico, the overthrow of Trujillo, and Panamanian control of the Panama Canal. But no independent-minded student in the world, much less in Latin America, would ever have disagreed on these points. The Congress quickly and unanimously proclaimed these points to be its program, then got down to work in small groups to decide how best to push for them.

One way was to convince other people. And so, Fidel and his friends started spending their non-Congress time distributing leaflets all over Bogotá. On April 3, 1948, they were severely beaten by the police for doing so in the city's main theatre.

Bogotá was a pretty hot place in those early days of April 1948. For almost a century before, Colombia had been ruled by the same kind of people: very rich landowners who also controlled the ports and, since the end of World War II, all the major industries as well; usually in partnership with such big American trusts as the Rockefellers, International Petroleum Corporation and International Basic Economy Corporation (IBEC). These people were known as "oligarchs." They still are. Today, Colombia's oligarchy, supported by U.S. advisers and integrated into the

U.S. economy, runs almost every aspect of the country's political, economic, and informational-cultural life.

To the outside world there are, and have always been, two oligarchies, grouped around two parties, the Conservative and the Liberal. And even if the people at the base vary in each party, it is the same oligarchy at the top of each. Indeed, since 1956, this has been clear even in Colombia's constitution which says that every four years the presidency of the country *must* alternate between the two parties.

In 1948, however, an accident had happened. A non-oligarch had become one of the undisputed leaders of the Liberal Party. His name was Jorge Eleicer Gaitán. He was not rich. And he was black. He was so popular, he was such a dynamic speaker, he was so sincerely *for* the poor and not the rich that it was clear he could lead the country into a complete overhaul of its decayed institutions. Young and old, student and illiterate, peasant and worker, everyone loved him—everyone, that is, except the members of the oligarchy. They, of course, feared him. And so, at a rally in Bogotá on April 9, 1948, they had him shot by a paid assassin whom the police, also on their orders, immediately killed so as to silence him.

The result was widespread riots. Everywhere the poor and the humble, students and workers went on a rampage. In the center of Bogotá, students tried to seize the capitol. Fidel and his friends were there. They decided to help.

Having obtained arms, they led the charge against the capitol and forced their way in. But in planning Gaitán's assassination, the oligarchy knew to expect riots. Its police were well prepared everywhere, and they had no trouble putting down the rebellion, which was spontaneous and disorganized. Fidel and Rafael just barely escaped. They rushed to the Cuban Embassy, then were smuggled out and flown back to Havana. "Still another defeat," said Fidel, "but this one was costly. Still we learned something important: No matter how many people are with you and how few the enemy are, organization is crucial. They will always have more guns and more money than us. Our task is to have not just better people—we'll always have that—but better planning."

On October 12, 1948, Fidel Castro married a fellow student, Mirtha Díaz Balart, from Oriente Province. By the following September, their son, Fidelito, was born. The new Castro family was very hard up financially. Mirtha's parents, very conservative people who hoped Fidel's idealism was just a youthful phase, didn't help. Angel Castro's aid became rarer and rarer as Fidel kept getting arrested for taking part in student protests and mass meetings.

But finally, in June 1950, Fidel graduated and became a lawyer. Immediately his practice was enormous. He didn't make much money. But he was constantly busy defending workers, farmers, and political prisoners.

In the next two years, Fidel became more and

more active politically. He ran for electoral posts, won some, lost some. Basically he was convinced that reforms could be worked out peacefully, through the ballot. He had joined Eduardo Chibas' Ortodoxo Party and had great faith in its leader. Indeed, Chibas was an able, intelligent, and courageous opponent of corruption. In Sunday-night radio talks, he was so daring in his outspoken denunciations of political crooks, whom he always named, that his vast audience was spellbound.

Fidel himself has talked about it:

"Chibas' party had once been very popular. Over the years landowners and opportunists had then seized most of its machinery. But faith in Chibas remained. People thought that once president he would get rid of these influence peddlers. I thought so too. I trusted his rebellious temperament, his personal honesty, and his feeling of obligation to the masses who supported him."

But Chibas lost his own faith. He decided he could never really change anything. So one Sunday, denouncing the stacked deck of Cuban politics, he ended his broadcast by committing suicide—on the air.

Fidel continues:

"Our people are so emotional that his death made them even more obligated to his party. Now there could be no doubt our party would win. But for me, it was a nightmare: the idea of all those opportunists coming to power. I reasoned that when deceived again, our people would become so skeptical, nothing could ever be done.

"But, meanwhile, I had gained some following myself and had gotten elected a deputy from Havana. Then I used my parliamentary mailing privilege, as I didn't have money for stamps, to mail eighty thousand letters each month—to stir things up, to propose new programs, to mobilize people—farmers, workers, intellectuals—behind new goals. I was already working with the fervent passion of a revolutionary. But I was still in the system. In fact I was up for election, and so was my party. We were going to win, that was for sure. I was aiming for later, for after the election. I wanted to cause a break in my party so that people would not just be deceived by the whole machinery, but would have to choose between us—the good guys—and them, the opportunists."

But the election of June 1, 1952, never took place. On March 10, Batista seized power with the Army. Fidel immediately denounced him as an usurper. He even went to court with a brief showing Batista had violated six articles of the constitution's Code of Social Defense, which was punishable by 108 years in jail. But the Court of Constitutional Guarantees rejected Fidel's brief. Batista came to power through revolution, said the court, and "revolution is the fount of law"—meaning the constitution no longer applies.

3

"After Batista seized power," said Fidel, "I just wanted to be a soldier. I started organizing action cells. I hoped all the leaders of constitutional parties would lead the action. All I wanted was a rifle to do my duty. But not one of those leaders came forward. So I started to work out a strategy of my own.

"We had no money for guns. But I told my comrades we didn't need any. There were plenty of weapons, well-oiled modern weapons, inside Batista's stockades. All we had to do was seize one of them, then distribute the guns to the people.

"Word of our activity leaked out. But young men had talked about revolution and done nothing for so long that no one took us seriously at first. Just more propaganda, they said. But we were dead serious."

By the time the government believed it, Fidel and his friends were training in secret. With their personal savings they had bought weapons, mostly .22 rifles. They considered themselves an army, a revolutionary army, and so obtained uniforms as well. Unfortunately, these uniforms were made of the same material as those worn by Batista's army, which meant they were the same color. That, later, proved to be a mistake.

Fidel's army was made up of some 150 soldiers, including a few women. Their goal was to seize the Moncada Barracks, Cuba's second biggest military fortress, just on the outskirt of Santiago. Fidel's plan was relatively simple: Through lightning-fast strikes by small columns, they would first seize various government buildings (hospitals, radio station, etc.) in Santiago and nearby Bayamo, then by direct assault two commando forces of almost fifty men each would seize Moncada, take the one thousand soldiers quartered there by surprise, capture their machine guns, tanks, and ammunition. Immediately the radio would ask the Cuban people to support the insurrection.

The attack—on July 26, 1953—failed. Fidel himself will describe why in a moment. But very few of his men were killed in the battle. Most were tracked down in the next few days. They were tortured and killed. Scores of innocent people died too. Batista's police and soldiers, under orders to kill ten men for each government soldier killed, shot at anything. They roamed the streets of Santiago and unleashed gusts of machine-gun bullets at anything which moved, often children.

In 1961, Esteva Llora remembered that day. She was now head of education at Moncada Barracks, which Fidel had turned into a learning institute. On

July 26, 1953, she was an ordinary teacher who had never heard of Fidel Castro. She was woken up by the sounds of the machine guns. "'Who are these young men?' everyone asked. 'Who are these boys?' Nobody knew. My husband heard that neighbors were trying to hide the wounded. We ourselves found four. We saved their lives. But the others, those captured, they were killed. They were tied up and lined up right there at that parking lot, and machine-gunned."

There was no free press in Cuba. Censorship was rigid. But the story of the massacres would not be stilled. Too many families in Santiago saw what had happened. They protested. Finally Monsignor Perez Serantes, Archbishop of Santiago, intervened. He got a promise from the commanding general of the city that no one else would be killed, if they surrendered. But the general told his men: "Except Fidel Castro. Kill *him!*"

But luck was with Fidel this time. The patrol that discovered him and two comrades, exhausted, was made up of men who didn't recognize him. Except their leader, Lieutenant Pedro Sarria, and he had been a student in Havana at the same time as Fidel. Leaning over as if to check for weapons, Sarria whispered to Fidel: "Don't give your right name or you will be shot."

With Fidel in jail, Raúl Castro and his men, who had been hiding in the mountains, came down and surrendered. Most of Fidel's soldiers were now either dead or captured. Batista had to put on a show trial, to convince the world that he respected democratic procedures.

The trial began in September 1953 with 122 prisoners, many of whom had nothing to do with the July 26 attack. All approaches to the courthouse were blocked by armored cars except for the main artery connecting it with the jail. That artery was lined with one thousand soldiers, machine guns at the ready. All prisoners except Fidel were transported by buses. Fidel was brought by jeep, handcuffed to the vehicle and escorted by heavily armed soldiers in other jeeps on all four sides.

Batista hoped for a quick trial. To fool the press he allowed three regular judges, though working for him, to preside. The trouble was these judges knew the law, even that little bit of the law Batista was willing to use. And according to that law, Fidel Castro, as a lawyer, was not only allowed to defend himself but to cross-examine witnesses. And so Fidel began by delivering one of the most memorable speeches ever given, a speech that is known today throughout the world as "History Will Absolve Me."

It was a very long speech so we cannot let Fidel speak it, here and now, in full. But let us hear him as, standing proudly in front of the three judges, he explained what happened on that famous day, July 26, 1953.

"The government said the attack showed such precision and perfection that military strategists must

31

have done the planning. Nothing could be further from the truth. The plan was prepared by a group of young men none of whom had any military experience . . .

"Much more difficult than planning the attack was our organizing, training, mobilizing, and arming men under this repressive regime with its millions of dollars spent on espionage, bribery, and information.

"The attack was carried out with magnificent coordination. It began simultaneously at 5:15 A.M. in both Bayamo and Santiago de Cuba; and one by one, with an exactitude of minutes and seconds prepared in advance, the buildings surrounding the barracks fell to our forces. Nevertheless, in the interest of accuracy and even though it may detract from our reputation, I am also going to reveal a fact that was fatal: Due to a most unfortunate error, half of our forces, and the better armed half at that, went astray at the entrance to the city and were not on hand to help us at the decisive moment.

"Abel Santamaría, with twenty-one men, had occupied the City Hospital; with him went a doctor and two of our women comrades to attend the wounded. Raúl Castro, with ten men, occupied the Palace of Justice, and it was my responsibility to attack the barracks with the rest, ninety-five men. Preceded by an advance guard of eight who had forced Gate Three, I arrived with the first group of forty-five men.

"It was precisely here that the battle began, when

an automobile ran into a perimeter patrol armed with machine guns. The reserve group, who had almost all the heavy weapons (the light arms were in the advance guard), turned up the wrong street and lost their way in the city, with which they were not familiar. I must clarify that I do not for a moment doubt the valor of those men; they experienced great anguish and desperation when they realized they were lost. Because of the type of action under way and because of the identical color of the uniforms of the two contending forces, it was not easy for these men to re-establish contact with us. Many of them, captured later on, met death with true heroism . . .

"In reflecting on the causes for our tactical failure, apart from the regrettable error already mentioned, I believe we made a mistake by dividing the commando unit we had so carefully trained. Of our best trained men and boldest leaders, there were twenty-seven in Bayamo, twenty-one in the City Hospital, and ten in the Palace of Justice . . .

"The clash with the patrol alerted the camp and gave them time to mobilize. Otherwise the camp would have fallen without a shot since the guard post was already in our control. On the other hand, except for the .22 caliber rifles, for which there were plenty of bullets, our side was very short of ammunition. Had we had hand grenades, the Army would not have been able to resist us for fifteen minutes.

"When I became convinced that all efforts to take

33

the barracks had become quite futile, I began to withdraw our men in groups of eight and ten. Our retreat was covered by six expert marksmen under the command of Pedro Miret and Fidel Labrador; heroically they impeded the Army's advance. Our losses in the battle had been insignificant; 95 per cent of our casualties came from the Army's inhumanity after the struggle. The group in the City Hospital had but one casualty; the rest of that group were trapped when the troops blocked the only exit.

"Our plans were to continue the struggle in the mountains in case the attack on the regiment failed. In Siboney I was able to gather a third of our forces; but many of these men were now discouraged. About twenty of them decided to surrender . . .

"The rest, eighteen men, with what arms and ammunition were left, followed me into the mountains. The terrain was completely unknown to us. For one week we held the heights of the Gran Piedra range and the Army occupied the foothills. We could not come down and they did not decide to come up. It was not force of arms but hunger and thirst that ultimately overcame our resistance.

"I had to divide the men into smaller groups. Some managed to slip through the Army lines; others were escorted to be surrendered by Monsignor Perez Serantes. Finally, only two companions remained with me, José Suarez and Oscar Alcalde. While the the three of us were totally exhausted, a force led by Lieutenant Sarria surprised us in our sleep at dawn.

This was Saturday, August 1. The slaughter of prisoners had ceased by then, as a result of tremendous protest by the people. This officer saved us from being murdered on the spot with our hands tied behind us.

"The soldiers were told that former President Prío had given us a million dollars; they were told this in the regime's attempt to distort the most important fact: that our movement had no link with politicians; that this movement is made up of a new Cuban generation, with its own ideas, rising up against tyranny; that this movement is made up of young men who were barely seven years old when Batista perpetrated the first of his crimes in 1934 . . .

"On July 27, in his speech from the military headquarters, Batista said that the assailants suffered thirty-two dead. At the end of the week, the number of dead had risen to more than eighty men. In what battles, where, in what clashes did these young men die? Before Batista spoke, more than twenty-five prisoners had been murdered. After Batista spoke, fifty more were murdered . . .

"Our men were killed not in the course of a minute, an hour or a day. Throughout a whole week the blows, the torture, and the shots continued. The Moncada Barracks were turned into a workshop of torture and death. The walls were splattered with blood. The bullets imbedded in the walls were encrusted with singed bits of skin, brains, and human hair, the grisly reminders of rifle shots full in the face.

The grass around the barracks was dark and sticky with human blood . . .

"The first prisoner killed was our doctor, Mario Muñoz, who bore no arms, wore no uniform, and was dressed in the white smock of a physician. He was a generous and able man who would have given to the wounded adversary the same devoted care as to a friend. On the road from the City Hospital to the barracks, they shot him in the back and left him lying there, face downward in a pool of blood. But the mass murders of prisoners did not begin until after three o'clock in the afternoon.

"It was then General Martín Díaz Tamayo arrived from Havana. He brought specific instructions from Batista, and from the head of the Army, the head of the Military Intelligence Service, and others. He said: 'It is humiliating and dishonorable for the Army to have lost in combat three times as many men as the insurgents did. Ten prisoners must be killed for each dead soldier.' This was his order . . .

"In the Centro Gallego Batista's men broke into the operating room at the very moment when two of our critically wounded were receiving blood transfusions. They pulled them off the tables and they dragged them down to the basement where they arrived as corpses.

"They could not do the same in the Spanish Clinic, where Gustavo Arcos and José Ponce were patients, because they were prevented from doing so by Dr.

Posada who bravely told them they could enter only over his dead body.

"Air and camphor were injected into the veins of Pedro Miret, Abelardo Crespo, and Fidel Labrador, in an attempt to kill them at the Military Hospital. They owed their lives to Captain Tamayo, an army doctor who, pistol in hand, wrenched them out of their merciless captors' grasp and transferred them to the City Hospital. These five young men were the only ones of our wounded to survive.

"In the early morning hours, groups of our men were removed from the barracks and taken in automobiles to Siboney, La Maya, Songo, and elsewhere. Then they were led out—tied, gagged, already disfigured by torture—and murdered in isolated spots . . .

"Few of the captured survived. Many were compelled to dig their own graves. One of our men, while he was digging, wheeled around and marked the face of one of his assassins with his pick. Others were buried alive, their hands tied behind their backs . . .

"In Bayamo, three victims were removed from the Manzanillo Barracks at two o'clock in the morning. They were taken to a particular spot on the highway, beaten until they were unconscious, and strangled with ropes. After they were abandoned, given up for dead, one of them, Andrés García, regained consciousness and took refuge in the house of a farmer. Thanks to this, he is now here and the court has learned the details of this crime. Of all our men taken prisoner in the Bayamo area, this boy was the only survivor."

Fidel went on to describe the murders of seventy more of his compatriots. Naturally, Batista was very upset by this performance. He could not allow it to continue. And so, on the third day of the trial, Fidel did not show up at the courthouse. "He is sick," explained the chief of police.

"Mr. President," shouted a woman defendant, "Fidel Castro is not sick!" Her name was Melba Hernandez. She had participated in the Moncada Barracks attack. Her fiancé, one of Fidel's closest friends, had been one of those tortured and murdered.

"Here," she told the judge, "I bring you a letter from Dr. Castro." She started searching in her hair and pulled out a tiny roll of paper. "As you can see, it is in Dr. Castro's own handwriting and it is addressed to this honorable court," she said handing over the note.

The judge unrolled the paper and read the letter. In it Fidel said he was not at all sick and that the police were planning to kill him.

From that day on, all the prisoners were searched from head to foot before each session. Melba Hernandez was put in solitary confinement. Fidel, already in such confinement, was sent to the most inaccessible part of the prison. But two court-appointed doctors did get to examine him.

They said he was perfectly healthy. The court ordered him to appear. But the police refused to obey the court. Still, the maneuver saved Fidel's life, for now the police did not dare kill him.

The trial ended in October. Fidel was sentenced to fifteen years in jail. Raúl got thirteen years. They were sent to the infamous prison island, the Isle of Pines.

4

For seven months, Fidel was kept in solitary confinement on the Isle of Pines. When he was finally allowed to mix with other prisoners, he immediately set up a prison school and taught the others what he knew about history, politics, and philosophy. Some of the other prisoners taught too. The school was so successful that the morale became too good to satisfy the police. They broke it up and put Fidel back in the hole—solitary confinement.

But then Batista thought he would try to win an election. So he lifted the censorship laws. Suddenly every Cuban newspaper and magazine was free to talk about Moncada and the trial—but not the tortures. And so they did, in gaudy front-page stories.

Batista was in trouble again. There were strikes everywhere, even illegal demonstrations. On the wall of the Malecón, that long, beautiful road that borders Havana's shoreline, appeared one day a four-foot-tall sign: "July 26, 1953." Batista tried to ignore all this and scheduled "free" elections for November

1954. But whenever candidates rose to speak inevitably the crowds chanted: "Free Fidel!" and "Viva Fidel!" Batista had to eliminate such opposition. He ran for President and won. But he allowed no one to oppose him.

In February 1955, as he inaugurated himself to a "new" four-year term, resentment against him was at an all-time high. "Free Fidel and get rid of those symbols," his advisers told him. Even the Cuban Bar Association, which traditionally was very reactionary, pressured Batista to grant Fidel an amnesty. Officials everywhere told him it was the only way to smother the discontent.

Batista yielded. He ordered a journalist to pose the question of an amnesty directly to Fidel. But Fidel answered: "After twenty months we are as firm and unmoved as on the first day. We do not want an amnesty at the price of dishonor."

By then Batista had no choice: He had to free Fidel and his troops without imposing conditions. He finally did so on May 15, 1955.

The release of Fidel and his comrades was a day of rejoicing. On the Isle of Pines the festivities lasted until the boat sailed. (Fidel was greeted by one of his sisters; his wife, whose brother was a close friend of Batista's, had deserted him.) In Havana the next day, their train was met by all the major opposition leaders, including Raúl Chibas, Eduardo's brother. University students sang the Cuban national anthem; then, carrying Fidel aloft on their shoulders,

41

paraded him through the streets. Everywhere the shouts were "Viva Fidel!" "Viva the 26th of July."

For a while Fidel set up shop in Vedado, Havana's fancy new district. He was in no way a repentant prisoner, but a proud revolutionary leader who told everyone he would soon begin anew. Then he left for Mexico, declaring he was off to find arms and would return to liberate Cuba. His comrades from Moncada rushed to join him.

In Mexico, Fidel behaved like the exiled head of a sister country on an official visit. He laid flowers on the tombs of Mexican revolutionary heroes. He made speeches at the university, at cultural institutes, even at business centers. He kept popping up everywhere, collecting funds, making contacts, keeping the Mexican police tail constantly on the go.

From Cuba, Batista fretted. He stopped maligning the Communists. He even stopped harassing Chibas' Ortodoxo Party, many of whose members were now working for Fidel in the 26th of July Movement (M-26). Batista concentrated his propaganda on Fidel, thus making him the most famous of his opponents. "The biggest mistake of Batista's life," rejoiced Fidel.

Fidel also went to America. He canvassed the rich exiles, talking to anyone who would listen, and came back to Mexico with fifty thousand dollars. Now he could buy arms and train his army—which had grown to more than eighty. Fidel also found a teacher: Colonel Alberto Bayo, then sixty-three, a Cuban revolutionary who had fought with the guerrillas for Moroccan independence and had served with the Loyalist forces in Spain, in the civil war against Franco.

Bayo found a good place in the Mexican mountains, a site surrounded by jungle. Fidel and his men moved up there and trained intensely for three months. They learned to become marksmen with all kinds of weapons, to use first aid and camouflage, and to blow up targets with make-do material. They went on forced marches for five, ten, fifteen hours a day, crawled, swam, ran with full packs, learned to harass the enemy, attack and withdraw, survive on the fruits of the earth. Most important, they learned discipline and comradeship.

Bayo gave Fidel's men grades. No. 1 was not even a Cuban. He was an Argentine named Ernesto Guevara. As is the habit in Argentine slang, Guevara called everyone "Che"—meaning "Hey, Mac." The Cubans liked that, so they nicknamed him "Che," Che Guevara.

Che was a doctor who suffered from asthma. But he was a dedicated revolutionary. He had seen too much poverty, too much exploitation to believe that a doctor could do very much until justice was established first. Che had tried to help the social revolution in Guatemala in 1954, but after it was crushed by U.S.-trained and financed mercenaries and CIA planes, he had fled to Mexico and was barely managing to eat as a tourist photographer. Then he met

43

Raúl Castro, who introduced him to Fidel. The three immediately became close friends and Che joined Fidel's army—as a soldier, not a doctor. Now he was No. 1.

In *Reminiscences of the Cuban Revolutionary War*, Che told the story of what happened next: "At the time, two Mexican police forces, both paid by Batista, were hunting for Fidel. One had the good fortune to capture him as he was speeding to the ranch in a car full of guns. But they made a mistake; they didn't kill him."

The ranch was raided and, as Che put it, "We all went to jail. Some of us spent fifty-seven days in prison. It was precious time lost. But never did we lose our personal trust in Fidel Castro. For Fidel did some things which we might almost say compromised his revolutionary attitude for the sake of friendship. I remember making my own case clear: I was a foreigner, in Mexico illegally, and with a series of charges against me. I told Fidel that under no circumstances should the Revolution be held back for me; that he could leave me behind; that I understood the situation and would try to join their fight from wherever I was sent; that the only effort they should make on my behalf was to have me sent to a nearby country and not to Argentina. I remember Fidel's brusque reply: 'I will not abandon you.' And so it was, for they had to use precious time and money to get us out of the Mexican jail. The personal attitude of Fidel toward the people he esteems is the key to the absolute devotion which is created around him; loyalty to the man, together with an attachment to principles, make this rebel army an indivisible unit.

"The days passed, we worked secretly, hid where we could, avoided public appearances as much as possible, and in fact almost never went out into the street.

"When a few months had passed, we found there was a traitor in our ranks. We did not know who it was, but he had sold an arms shipment of ours. We also knew that he had sold the yacht and a transmitter. The first betrayal proved to the Cuban authorities that their agent was doing his job and knew our secrets. This is also what saved us, for we were shown the same thing. From that moment on, frenzied activity was necessary: our yacht, the *Granma*, was prepared with extraordinary speed, and we stocked it with as much food as we could get, as well as uniforms, rifles, equipment, and two anti-tank rifles with almost no ammunition."

Then, on November 15, 1956, as the *Granma* was almost set to sail, Fidel publicly—and very loudly—announced his intention to invade Cuba and overthrow Batista.

Colonel Bayo was furious. "One of the most important points you were supposed to have learned during training," he shouted at Fidel, "was to always keep your plans secret from the enemy."

Fidel smiled. "Yes, you taught me that," he replied, "but in this case I want everyone in Cuba to know I'm coming. I want them to have faith in the 26th of July Movement. It is a peculiarity all my own. I know that militarily it might be harmful. It is psychological warfare."

Ten days later, the *Granma*, with its army of eighty-two men, loaded with guns, medicine, ammunition was on its way. It was supposed to land at Niquero, a bit west of Santiago, on November 30. It was supposed to be met there by Cresencio Perez, a rebel farmer, with trucks and a hundred men. Its landing was supposed to coincide with massive uprisings in Holguín, Matanzas, Santiago, and other places, led by Frank País, a good friend of Fidel's and head of the 26th of July Movement inside Cuba. A few days later, a general strike was supposed to paralyze the country. Within a short time Batista was supposed to run off, knowing he was lost. Supposed to . . . That was the plan. But none of it worked.

The *Granma*, a fifty-eight-foot yacht designed for eight passengers and crew but loaded with eighty-two men, arms, supplies, extra gasoline, and with its clutch slipping, left on schedule. But then? Here's how Che told the story:

"With our lights extinguished we left the port of Tuxpan amid an infernal mess of men and all sorts of material. The weather was very bad and navigation was forbidden, though the river's estuary was calm. We crossed its mouth and [sailed] into the Gulf and a little later turned on our lights. We began a frenzied search for the anti-seasickness pills, which we did not find. We sang the Cuban national anthem and the 'Hymn of the 26th of July' for perhaps five minutes, and then the entire boat took on an aspect both ridiculous and tragic; men with anguished faces holding their stomachs, some with their heads in buckets, others lying in the strangest positions, immobile, their clothing soiled with vomit.

"Apart from two or three sailors and four or five other people, the rest of the eighty-two crew members were seasick. But by the fourth or fifth day the general panorama had improved a little. We discovered that what we had thought was a leak in the boat was actually an open plumbing faucet. We had thrown overboard everything superfluous in order to lighten the load . . .

"On the thirtieth, we heard over the radio the news of riots in Santiago de Cuba, which our great Frank País had organized, hoping to coincide with the arrival of our expedition. The following night, December 1, without water, fuel, and food, we were pointing our bow on a straight course toward Cuba, desperately seeking the lighthouse at Cabo Cruz. At two in the morning, on a dark and tempestuous night, the situation was really worrisome."

On December 2, the man at the wheel fell overboard. The choppy water and darkness made it impossible to locate him right away, so Fidel ordered the *Granma* to turn on its lights and circle. It was another two hours before the yacht could go on—with the lost navigator safely retrieved. But then, near a small fishing village not too far from Niquero, the *Granma* ran aground. Impossible to budge it.

Since it was near shore, Fidel told his men to forget the extra supplies, take what they could and get ashore. A wise move, for within a few minutes a spotter cutter radioed their whereabouts to Batista's air force. By the time the planes came, all eighty-two men were safely hidden in the mangrove-covered swamps off Playa de las Colorados, and the bombs fell like duds in the shallow waters.

Fidel looked up and, with a disdainful wave toward the planes, quipped: "Look, they are terrified because they know that we have come to destroy them." Not every man felt so sure at that unhappy moment, having abandoned most of their needed supplies. But Fidel cheered them up just the same. The war, as ridiculous as it appeared at that moment, had begun.

5

Che tells what happened next:

"We took several hours to get through the swamp. We were delayed in this by the lack of experience and the irresponsibility of a comrade who had claimed he knew the way. We had had seven days of continual hunger and sickness at sea, now three days on land which were even more terrible. Exactly ten days after leaving Mexico, after a night's march interrupted by fainting, exhaustion, and rest stops, we reached a place known as Alegría de Pío . . .

"It was there, on December 5, 1956, that we were set upon by Batista's troops. Nothing remained of our equipment but a few rifles, cartridge belts, and some wet bullets. Our medical supplies had disappeared, our packs had for the most part been left in the swamps. The previous day we had walked by night along the border of the cane fields of the Niquero sugar mill. We satisfied our hunger and thirst by eating cane as we walked and, inexperienced as we were, we left the peelings behind. We found out years later that the enemy did not in fact need these careless clues to our presence since our guide, one of the principal traitors in the Revolution, brought them to us. The guide had been given the night off, an error we were to repeat several times during the war, until we learned that civilians of unknown background were always to be closely watched when we were in danger zones . . .

"At dawn on the fifth only a few of us could go a step farther; our exhausted men could walk only short distances, and then needed long rest . . .

"At noon we became aware of unusual activity. Piper Cub planes as well as other military and private aircraft began to circle in the vicinity. Some of our men were calmly cutting and eating cane as the planes passed overhead, without thinking how visible they were to the low-flying aircraft . . .

"Comrade [Faustino] Montane and I were leaning against a tree, talking about our respective children; we were eating our meager rations, when we heard a shot. In a matter of seconds a hurricane of bullets rained on the troop of eighty-two men. Near me a comrade named Arbentosa was walking toward the plantation. A burst of gunfire hit us both. I felt a terrible blow on the chest and another in the neck and was sure I was dead. Arbentosa, spewing blood from his nose, mouth, and an enormous wound from a .45 bullet, shouted, 'They've killed me!' From the ground I said to Faustino: 'They've got me!' . . .

"Still firing, Faustino glanced at me and told me it was nothing. But in his eyes I read my death sentence. Then Almeida came by. 'Move!' he shouted, 'let's get out of here.' I was slumped against a tree. I straightened out so as to be sitting erect, as if sitting at attention. My left side was paralyzed, or so it felt. 'What the hell are you doing?' Almeida shouted, firing in almost every direction. He too was wounded, in the leg. I thought of Saint Just, the French Revolutionary hero, Robespierre's brother. On his way to be executed he too had straightened out. 'To die proudly,' he had said. So I said to Almeida: 'I am going to die proudly.' He waved his gun in my face. 'You're not going to die proudly; I'm going to blow your face off unless you move.'

"I looked at him in amazement, then he started to laugh. I smiled. It hurt. My wounds really hurt, but I began to move. We walked until night. We huddled together, attacked by mosquitoes, tortured by thirst and hunger, and pain. But we survived, five of us, Ramiro Valdés, Almeida, Chao, Benitez, and me, we had survived our first battle—our first defeat."

The others didn't fare much better—and some not at all. The group under Manuel Marquez, for example, never got out of the trap. They were promised prisoner-of-war status. So, thirteen of them plus Marquez surrendered. They were killed.

51

Many others were killed. Fidel was almost totally cut off from his men. With Universo Sanchez and Faustino Perez, he managed to hide out in a sugar-cane field for five days, with only the cane to munch on, no water. Only after five days did Batista's soldiers leave the area, and Fidel could move.

For Raúl and his men—Ciro Redondo, René Rodriguez, and Efigenio Almejeiras—it was even worse: eight days without food and water, except cane juice. Then, when the soldiers left, they found a cave in the foothills of the mountains, but couldn't move because they heard noise not too far away.

That noise came from Fidel's group. And they too heard noise. Like Raúl, Fidel thought the "other" noise was the enemy. So the two groups didn't unite for three days—until a peasant convinced each side.

Now they were seven! They had reached the Sierra Maestra, that formidable mountain range where it would be very difficult for Batista's soldiers to find them. Fidel was delighted. "The days of the dictatorship are numbered!" he shouted with confidence.

Rodriguez looked at him with utter amazement. "This man is crazy," he said to himself, "stark raving mad. Seven survivors from eighty-two, and he says we're winning. We've got no food, no contacts, no bullets almost, and he says we're winning. He's mad!!"

But there were more than seven survivors. Che has told how they all finally got together:

52

"Almeida and I suddenly noticed that in one of the little shanties that fishermen put up at the sea's edge to protect themselves from bad weather, there were shadows of sleeping men. We were sure they were soldiers, but we were already too close to retrace our steps. We strode ahead. Almeida was going to demand that they surrender, but we had a happy surprise: They were three comrades from the *Granma*, Camilo Cienfuegos, Pancho Gonzalez, and Pablo Hurtado. At once we began to exchange impressions, news, opinions about the little each of us knew concerning the other comrades and the battle. Camilo's group offered us sticks of sugar cane, which they had pulled up before fleeing . . .

"We trekked on, all together. The surviving combatants of the *Granma* army numbered eight at that point, and we had no information about the existence of other survivors! We thought that, according to all logic, there must be other groups such as ours. But we hadn't the least idea of where to find them. All we knew was that by marching with the sea to our right we were going east, that is, toward the Sierra, where we were to take refuge. We did not try to hide from ourselves the fact that in the case of an encounter with the enemy, trapped as we were between the craggy cliffs and the sea, our chances of flight were nil . . .

"Four days later, after much groping, we came upon a famous torrent that empties into the sea. Throwing ourselves to the ground, we drank for a long time. At dawn, we reached the top of a hillock crowned with a clump of trees. So that we could resist and hide most effectively, the group spread out; we spent the entire day watching small planes equipped with loudspeakers emitting incomprehensible noises as they buzzed us. Almeida and Benitez, veterans of Moncada, realized that they were calling on us to surrender . . .

"We took up our march but the men balked at every turn. That night, or perhaps it was the next one, all the comrades with few exceptions decided that they did not want to continue. We were obliged, at that moment, to knock at the door of a peasant near the road nine days after the surprise attack at Alegria de Pio.

"We were warmly received. That peasant hut became the scene of endless feasting. Hours passed and yet we ate, so much and so well that dawn found us still reveling. It was impossible to leave. During the morning there was a constant procession of peasants who, filled with curiosity and solicitude, came to make our acquaintance, offer us food, or bring us some gift.

"Then, the little house that sheltered us turned into an inferno. Almeida was the first to be overcome by diarrhea; and, in a flash, eight unappreciative intestines gave evidence of the blackest ingratitude. Some of the comrades began to vomit. Pablo Hurtado, exhausted by seasickness, by days of marching, by thirst and hunger, could no longer stand.

"We decided to leave that night. The peasants told us that according to the news they had picked up, Fidel was alive. They proposed to take us to a place where, in all probability, we could find him and Cresencio Perez. But they made one condition: we must leave our weapons and uniforms behind. Almeida and I kept our two-star Tommy guns. The eight guns and all the cartridges stayed in the peasant's hut as security. We planned to make it to the Maestra in stages, stopping over with peasants; we therefore divided into two groups, one of three men, one of four.

"Our group was composed of Pancho Gonzalez, Ramiro Valdés, Almeida, and myself. In the other were Camilo, Benitez, and Chao. Pablo Hurtado was too sick to leave the house.

"We were scarcely on our way when the owner gave in to the temptation of passing on the news to a friend. The latter convinced him to sell (our arms). They haggled with a third thief, and it was he who denounced us to the police. As a result, a few hours after our departure from the first hospitable Cuban hearth, there was an enemy raid; they took Pablo Hurtado prisoner and seized our weapons.

"We were staying with Argelio Rosabal. This comrade, hearing the bad news, promptly got in touch with another peasant who knew the zone thoroughly and was a rebel sympathizer. That same night we left for another safer shelter. The peasant whom we met on that occasion was Guillermo García: today he is the commander of the Oriente army . . .

"One morning we reached the farm of Mongo Perez, Cresencio's brother. There we found all the comrades of our landing troop who had survived and who were, for the time being, free: Fidel Castro, Universo Sanchez, Faustino Perez, Raúl Castro, Ciro Redondo, Efigenio Almejeiras, René Rodriguez, and Armando Rodriguez, who had also found his way to Fidel . . .

"Our little band was without uniforms and without weapons. In fact, aside from the two Tommy guns, we had salvaged nothing from the disaster. Fidel reproached us bitterly . . .

"He said: 'You have not paid for the error you committed, because the price you pay for the abandonment of your weapons under such circumstances is your life. The one and only hope of survival that you would have had, in the event of a head-on encounter with the Army, was your guns. To abandon them was criminal and stupid.' He was very angry. And he was right."

Fifteen men from eighty-two had survived the trap. Of the others all were dead, either killed in battle or executed after being made prisoners—except for ten, who were imprisoned on the Isle of Pines.

But six members of the 26th of July Movement

soon joined Fidel. And the revolutionary army had picked up its first peasant recruit: Guillermo García.

"I met Fidel for the first time on December 12, ten days after he landed in the *Granma*," García said later. "I remember the moment very well. We were walking through a banana field. Fidel said 'Are we already in the Sierra Maestra?' I said, 'Yes.' 'Then the Revolution has triumphed.'

"Did I believe him? If I didn't believe him I wouldn't be here now."

Eventually García became commander in chief of the army of the three western provinces and one of the original eleven members of the political bureau of Cuba's new Communist Party. "You know, Fidel spoke with so much emotion, you had to believe him. Even in that banana field, though it seemed crazy, I believed him."

For the next few days, Fidel worked hard just to secure a base. He found couriers, arranged for buying food (the M-26 always paid for what they took from the poor), got Che, Almeida, and the others treated for their wounds. Then he called over Faustino Perez. "I want you to go to Havana," Fidel said, "and take over the movement there. Get it going. Get us money, arms, explosives, supplies, recruits. Our network has not been functioning very well. Probably it's because Batista's censorship has the press saying we were wiped out, all dead."

Faustino went immediately. But before he left, he told Fidel: "Bury yourself in a hole and don't move.

The only thing that counts for us is that you stay alive. You symbolize the Revolution; we will do the rest in Havana."

Fidel thanked him, but had no such intention. Instead, he called for Frank País to come to see him.

Frank went with Haydee Santamaría, one of the two women who had taken part in the actual assault on the Moncada and who was now chief liaison for the M-26. "We must find a way of getting Fidel out of this," Frank said to Haydee on the way to the Sierra Maestra. "He must go to another country in Latin America and reorganize the movement. He could get killed here and we cannot afford the luxury."

Haydee remembers that day well. "Fidel just looked at us and said: 'Look, just get us guns and bullets. The soldiers are shooting down there but they never dare come up. If you get me the stuff, in two months we start the real battle.' There was such conviction, neither Frank nor I said anything. We just nodded and did as he wished."

One of Faustino Perez's instructions had been to get some famous journalist down to the Sierra Maestra. That way, Fidel thought, Batista's censorship would be broken on a world-wide front. Herbert Matthews of the New York *Times* was chosen as the journalist. Faustino got him down there.

When Fidel heard that Matthews had arrived, he told his men: "I want you to look like soldiers. Really put it on." The soldiers looked at each other.

Their clothes were ripped. Their shoes full of holes and tied with pieces of electrical wire. "But we managed," said one of them. Then, while Fidel was talking to Matthews, Raúl devised a little plot. He sent one of the men to Fidel. "Excuse me, Commander," the man said, "we have just affected liaison with the Second Column." "Fine!" said Fidel. He had to explain. So he calmly told Matthews that this was the general staff headquarters of the First Column and that there were others scattered throughout the Sierra Maestra. The truth, of course, was that Matthews was looking at the whole rebel army.

It worked. Matthews wrote various stories on the rebel army for the *Times*, and they were reprinted across the world. This is what Matthews wrote, in part:

"Fidel Castro, the rebel leader of Cuba's youth, is alive and fighting hard and successfully in the rugged, almost impenetrable vastnesses of the Sierra Maestra . . .

"President Fulgencio Batista has the cream of his Army around the area, but the Army men are fighting a thus-far losing battle to destroy the most dangerous enemy General Batista has yet faced . . .

"[Because of censorship] Havana does not and cannot know that thousands of men and women are heart and soul with Fidel Castro and the new deal for which they think he stands. It does not know that hundreds of highly respected citizens are helping Señor Castro, that bombs and sabotage are con-

59

stant, that a fierce Government counterterrorism has aroused the populace even more against President Batista . . .

"Fidel Castro and his 26th of July Movement are the flaming symbol of this opposition to the regime. The organization, which is apart from the university students' opposition, is formed of youths of all kinds. It is a revolutionary movement that calls itself socialistic. It is also nationalistic, which generally in Latin America means anti-Yankee . . .

"To arrange for me to penetrate the Sierra Maestra and meet Fidel Castro, dozens of men and women in Havana and Oriente Province ran a truly terrible risk. They must, of course, be protected with the utmost care in these articles for their lives would be forfeit—after the customary torture—immediately if any could be traced . . .

"From the look of things, General Batista cannot possibly hope to suppress the Castro revolt . . .

"[At the camp], one man told me how he had seen his brother's store wrecked and burned by government troops and his brother dragged out and executed. 'I'd rather be here fighting for Fidel than anywhere in the world now,' he said . . .

"The personality of [Fidel] is overpowering. It was easy to see that his men adored him and also to see why he has caught the imagination of the youth of Cuba all over the island. Here was an educated, dedicated fanatic, a man of ideals, of courage and of remarkable qualities of leadership.

"As the story unfolded of how he had at first gathered the few remnants of the 82 around him, one got the feeling that he is now invincible. Perhaps he isn't, but that is the faith he inspires in his followers . . .

"Castro is a great talker. His brown eyes flash; his intense face pushed close to the listener and the whispering voice, as in a stage play, lends a vivid sense of drama.

"'We have been fighting for 79 days now and are stronger than ever,' Señor Castro said. 'The [government] soldiers are fighting badly; their morale is low and ours could not be higher. We are killing many but when we take prisoners, they are never shot. We question them, talk kindly to them, take their arms and equipment and then set them free . . .'

"'I have followers all over the island. All the best elements, especially all the youth, are with us. The Cuban people will stand anything but oppression,' he said. 'Cuba is in a state of war, but Batista is hiding it. A dictatorship must show that it is omnipotent or it will fall; we are showing that it is important . . .'

"'I am always in the front line,' he said; and the others confirmed the fact. Such being the case, the Army might yet get him, but in present circumstances he seems almost invulnerable.

"'They never know where we are,' he said . . . 'but we always know where they are . . .'"

Later in another article, Matthews added:

"There is also bitter criticism in Cuba, as in all Latin American dictatorships, over the sale of U.S. arms. While I was there, 7 tanks were delivered in a ceremony headed by [U.S.] Ambassador Gardner. Every Cuban I spoke with saw the delivery as arms furnished to General Batista for use in bolstering his regime and for use 'against the Cuban people.'"

The Matthews interviews were like an explosion. They were carried on U.S. radio. And since Cuba is only ninety miles off the coast, every Cuban who listened to the radio heard them.

The articles forced Batista, furious, to make another bad blunder. Instead of ignoring them or laughing them off, he denied them. He called them "a chapter in a fantastic novel," and claimed that there was no rebel army and Fidel was not in Cuba. The New York *Times* then simply published photographs of Matthews and Fidel in the Sierra Maestra.

The effect was stupendous. New recruits began to arrive in the Sierra almost daily. Money, guns, ammunition began to flow in. Fidel was very pleased; his plot had worked.

But Matthews never regretted having been fooled. He wrote, years later:

"I did not know how small a force Fidel had at that time—18 men with rifles—but I doubt that this would have made any difference in the story I wrote for the New York *Times*. The dangerous position we were in during my interview was perfectly obvious. In fact, all through the morning, we had to talk in whispers and every one of the group was under orders not to speak in a normal voice. We were surrounded by Batista's soldiers. One of my most vivid recollections of the incident is of Fidel crouching on the ground next to me and of his hoarse, impassioned whisper in my left ear as he poured his youthful revolutionary heart out . . .

"[Fidel] knew he needed publicity; he always had a keen eye for that, and this was one of his most brilliant strokes . . . the word had gone out that Castro was killed at the time of the *Granma* landing. Fidel wanted to prove that he was alive and fighting . . .

"It has become a standard source of glee among the Cuban rebels who were there . . . that they had fooled me into believing that they were a larger and stronger force than they really were. [In New York in 1959] Fidel himself, with a slightly malicious gleam in his eyes, broke the news that he had only 18 armed men. [But I was convinced] that so long as Castro fought the way he did in that trackless mountain jungle, Batista's troops could not destroy his guerrillas. The great risk was that Fidel would be killed while leading his men—and he always did lead them in those early months."

Fidel did more than lead in battle. He led all the time. He cared for his men, talked to them, inspired them, ironed out the inevitable differences which often separated one from another. And he studied, as Guillermo García said:

"There we were in the mountains, far away from civilization. We had no troops, no arms, no clothes, no food. Yet even then Fidel was always studying. We hadn't even started to fight the enemy, and Fidel was already analyzing international affairs. I remember we would be worrying about where we could find something to eat, and Fidel would be talking about America and Eisenhower and making plans for the future. He always had that way. He always analyzed the enemy's reaction in advance and prepared for it.

"Another thing. Fidel had never been in these mountains before. But in six months he knew the whole Sierra better than any *guajiro* [poor peasant] who was born here. He never forgot a place that he went to. He remembered everything—the soil, the trees, who lived in each house. In those days I was a cattle buyer. I used to go all over the mountains. But in six months, Fidel knew the Sierra better than I did, and I was born and raised here."

But now Batista knew he was in trouble. He sent more and more troops, and put a price of one hundred thousand dollars on Fidel's head—dead or alive.

6

The rebel army had to stay on the move. Fidel himself set the pace, beginning at six in the morning and stopping after nightfall, about eight. As one soldier wrote: "We usually waded across several rivers or sometimes the same river in different places, without stopping except for a few minutes every two hours or so for coffee. When we pitched camp, our swollen feet refused to come out of our boots, which were still soaking wet. Sometimes, but very rarely for security reasons, Fidel would accept the invitation of some guajiro to share their meal and stay in their house. When he did, he always made sure that a one-hundred-peso note was pressed into the guajiro's hand when we left."

It was then, too, that Fidel ordered his men to grow beards, so that guajiros would not be taken as rebels and killed. Soon beards became such a powerful symbol that a Batista soldier on leave who had let his beard grow was machine-gunned and killed by police in the center of Santiago.

It was the guajiros, in those early days, who saved the revolutionaries from defeat. They constantly misled the Army, stole their arms and gave them to Fidel, and kept him informed as to the Army's movements. But until March 1957, there was not much Fidel and his tiny band could do except keep moving. "It got so bad," said Pedro Miret, a veteran of Moncada who joined Fidel when he got out of a Mexican jail, "that we finally put Fidel on a mule. Why? Because the mule walked slower than Fidel."

At the beginning of March, Frank País came up to the Sierra with fifty-odd men. They were green, soft, and for many it was too hard to be constantly moving, soaked, hungry, and exhausted. But others stuck it out and within a short time, Fidel was ready to attack with two groups of over twenty men each.

By then the whole country was in turmoil. On March 13, 1957, a group of students from Havana University's "Directorio" attacked the presidential palace and almost succeeded in killing Batista. They fought very bravely against the one-thousand-strong contingent of guards. But they failed. Their leader, José Antonio Echevarría, was killed. The second in command, Faure Chomón, escaped, and eventually he set up a second guerrilla front in the Sierra Escambray, in the center of Cuba.

But Batista's repression was so vicious that, though it scared many, it also forced many others to join the guerrillas. So Fidel finally ordered the first attack on the lowlands. It was a tiny battle, in comparison with what people expect in a war, but it was very important, for it built up morale and showed that the guerrillas were not restricted just to the impenetrable jungles of the high mountains. Che Guevara has described it thus:

"The attack on the small barracks at the mouth of the La Plata River in the Sierra Maestra brought us our first victory and had repercussions which reached far beyond the craggy region where it took place. It came to everyone's attention, proving that the rebel army existed and was ready to fight . . .

"We found out that there were about fifteen soldiers in the barracks; furthermore, we were told that in a while one of the three most infamous foremen in the region, Chicho Osorio, would pass along the road. After a while, Chicho appeared, drunk and mounted on a mule. Universo Sanchez called to him to halt in the name of the Guardia Rural . . .

"Despite our ragged appearance, we were able to trick Chicho Osorio, maybe because he was so drunk. Fidel, in an indignant manner, told him he was an Army colonel, that he had come to find out why the rebels had not yet been destroyed, that *he* was going into the mountains to find them (that was why he had a beard), and that what the Army was doing was 'garbage' . . .

"With great submissiveness, Chicho Osorio said that it was true, the guards spent their time inside

67

the barracks, eating and doing nothing but carry out unimportant maneuvers . . .

"We began to ask Chicho discreetly about friendly and unfriendly people in the region. In this way we collected about twenty names and the scoundrel continued jabbering. He told us that he had killed two men, 'but *mi general* Batista let me go free immediately'; he told us how he had just beaten some peasants who had 'gotten a bit uppity' . . .

"Fidel asked him what he would do with Fidel Castro if he captured him, and Chicho answered with an unmistakable gesture that he would cut off his genitals. 'Look,' he said, pointing to the Mexican-made boots he wore (and which we wore also), 'I got them off one of those sons of bitches we killed.' There, without knowing it, Chicho Osorio had signed his own death sentence. In the end, on Fidel's suggestion, he agreed to lead us to the barracks in order to surprise the soldiers and show them that they were poorly prepared and were neglecting their duty.

"We approached the barracks, with Chicho Osorio leading us; personally, I was not too sure that the man had not already caught on to our game. However, he continued in all innocence; he was so drunk his judgment was impaired. As we crossed the river once again in order to come closer to the barracks, Fidel told him that according to military regulations prisoners had to be bound; Chicho did not resist and he unknowingly continued as a real prisoner . . .

"Fidel started the shooting with two bursts of machine-gun fire and was followed by all the available guns. Immediately, we called on the soldiers to surrender, but with no result. The moment the shooting began, Chicho Osorio, the murdering informer, was executed . . .

"The casualty list was as follows: they had two dead and five wounded, and three of them were our prisoners. On our side, not even a scratch. We set the soldiers' houses on fire and withdrew, after attending to the wounded as best we could. There were three seriously wounded who subsequently died, as we found out after the final victory. We left them in the care of the captured soldiers. One of the soldiers later joined the troops of Major Raúl Castro and reached the rank of lieutenant . . .

"Our attitude with the wounded contrasted sharply with that of the Army. The Army not only murdered our wounded, but also abandoned their own. In time, this difference began having its effect, and constituted one of the factors in our victory. To my despair, Fidel ordered us to leave all our medicines with the prisoners who were to treat the wounded. We also freed the civilians."

That was the first victory. But there were many defeats. One was very costly. Fidel had sent Calixto Sanchez to Mexico to organize another landing. He did, with twenty-seven men aboard the *Corinthia*. But they were betrayed. As they landed, a group of soldiers dressed like guajiros and shouting, "Viva

Castro" came toward them, took them by surprise, and killed seventeen on the spot. The remaining ten did get away, and soon began sabotage operations in the area.

Then, on May 28, 1957, Fidel attacked a well-defended garrison post of sixty men at El Uvero, at the base of the Sierra Maestra, in broad daylight. "It was one of the bloodiest episodes of the war," said Che, "and it was a total victory for us." As a result, Batista pulled back his men from all isolated Sierra outposts, and the rebels now controlled the Sierra. The publicity brought new recruits and more weapons. One recruit became a symbol: Padre Guillermo Sardiñas, priest of Nueva Gerona parish, who became the revolutionaries' fighting chaplain.

That battle and others which rapidly followed convinced Fidel to issue his first proclamation to the people of Cuba on July 12, 1957. He asked for the unconditional support of all Cubans in overthrowing Batista.

But there were many serious defeats still in the offing. That month, in fact, Frank País was cornered and murdered in Santiago by the chief of police himself. Fidel later ordered that Frank be buried in the uniform of a colonel in the rebel army, a rank never attained by anyone else in the M-26 (Fidel, Raúl, Che, García, all remained *comandantes*, or majors, the highest rank to this day).

By the end of the year, the *barbudos* ("bearded ones," as the guerrillas began to be called) numbered one hundred. Fidel decided to break them up into two columns, and made Che commander of the second. "There was a certain tactical independence of command," Che said, "but we were under Fidel's orders and kept in touch with him every week or two by messenger."

Che continued:

"Organizationally, our guerrilla army had developed sufficiently to have, by the year's end, an elementary setup for provisions, certain minimal industrial services, hospitals, and communications services . . .

"In the beginning the small guerrilla units, some twenty men, would eat a meager ration of Sierra vegetables, chicken soup on holidays; sometimes the peasants provided a pig, for which they were scrupulously paid. As the guerrilla force grew and groups of pre-*guerrilleros* were trained, more provisions were needed. The Sierra peasants did not have cattle and generally theirs was a subsistence diet. They depended on the sale of their coffee to buy indispensable processed items such as salt. As an initial step we arranged with certain peasants that they should plant specified crops beans, corn, rice, etc.— which we guaranteed to purchase. At the same time we came to terms with certain merchants in nearby towns for the supplying of foodstuffs and equipment. Mule teams were organized, belonging to the guerrilla forces . . .

"The problem of supplying ourselves with arms

was another story. It was difficult to bring arms from the llano; to the natural difficulties of geographical isolation were added the arms requirements of the city forces themselves, and their reluctance to deliver them to the guerrillas. Fidel was constantly involved in sharp discussions in an effort to get equipment to us. The only substantial shipment made to us during that first year of struggle, except for what the combatants brought with them, was the remainder of the arms used in the attack on the palace . . .

"Certain sanitary regulations were established at this time, and the first hospitals were organized, one of them set up in the zone under my command in a remote, inaccessible place, offering relative security to the wounded, since it was invisible from the air. But since it was in the heart of a dense forest, its dampness made it unhealthy for the wounded and the sick. [Similar hospitals were organized for Fidel's column, which were improved during the second year of the struggle.]

"The troops' equipment needs such as cartridge boxes and belts, knapsacks, and shoes were met by a small leather-goods workshop set up in our zone. When we turned out the first army cap I took it to Fidel, bursting with pride. It caused quite an uproar; everyone claimed that it was a guaguero's [slang for "bus driver"] cap, a word unknown to me until then. The only one who showed me any mercy was a municipal councilor from Manzanillo, who was visiting the camp and who took it with him as a souvenir.

"Our most important industrial installation was a forge and armory, where defective arms were repaired and bombs, mines and the famous M-26 [Molotov cocktail] were made. At first the mines were made of tin cans and we filled them with material from bombs frequently dropped by enemy planes which had not exploded. These mines were very faulty. Later a comrade had the idea of using the whole bomb for major attacks, removing the detonator and replacing it with a loaded shotgun; we would pull the trigger from a distance by means of a cord, and this would cause an explosion. Afterward, we perfected the system, making special fuses of metal alloy and electric detonators. These gave better results . . .

"Later, Raúl in his new operations center created stronger industries than those we had during the first year of war. Our army's butcher shop was supplied with cattle which we confiscated from informers and latifundistas. We shared equitably, one part for the peasant population and one part for our troops.

"As for the dissemination of our ideas, first we started a small newspaper, *El Cubano Libre*. We had a mimeograph machine brought up to us from the lowlands, on which the paper was printed.

"By the end of the first year, we had a small radio transmitter. The first regular broadcasts were made

73

in February 1958; our only listeners were Palencho, a peasant who lived on the hill facing the station, and Fidel, who was visiting our camp in preparation for the attack on Pino del Agua. He listened to it on our own receiver. Little by little the technical quality of the broadcasts improved. It was then taken over by Column One, and by December 1958 had become one of the Cuban stations with the highest rating . . .

"All these small advances, including our equipment—such as a winch and some generators, which we laboriously carried up to the Sierra so as to have electric light—were due to our connections. Even the city bourgeoisie helped us. But, mostly, we were helped by the peasants."

In helping the barbudos, the guajiros also taught them a lesson—their own. The barbudos, who had never realized the extent of peasant misery, never forgot the lesson. They saw that in the Sierra Maestra region alone, some three hundred thousand human beings lived on the edge of society, nearly forgotten by the world, cultivating land belonging to others for almost no wage. Their children never went to school, never wore shoes, never saw a doctor. No one even knew what a hospital was—until the barbudos set one up. Later, when Raúl Castro set up a new front in the Sierra Cristal Mountains, he discovered that more than a million people lived the same way there.

In the beginning the guajiros only hid the rebels.

74

But gradually they began to help. The soldiers of the M-26 were different from the others. They were friendly and helpful. They paid for what they took. When they finally set up that first hospital, they cared for everyone and with the same good cheer. When Che opened the first school, they taught anyone who wanted to learn, not just peasants who fought with them. Before the war ended, thirty such schools were going full time.

And Fidel was a different kind of commander. He ate with his men, with peasants, with kids. He talked to them and explained endlessly and with passion and love what he hoped to achieve.

In return, the peasants learned to love Fidel and his men. They joined his army. They carried the supply trains. But not just the peasants. Office workers and secretaries led a double life, doing their jobs in the daytime, revolutionary work at night. They sabotaged trains, military depots, government buildings. They printed and distributed leaflets. They sold "freedom bonds" and sent Fidel the money. In Havana, they dynamited the gas and electricity mains, once paralyzing the city for fifty-four hours. They cut telephone lines.

One journalist told this story:

"In Santiago a young soldier came walking down the street one evening—in his shorts. His hands were tied behind his back, but in one he held his wallet. 'Four civilians jumped me and robbed me!' he shouted. 'Well, they didn't exactly rob me. They gave me back my money. They said they didn't want to deprive me personally but that they were taking away the people's property—my uniform, boots, guns, ammunition, and grenades.' The rebels obviously had a new supply sergeant—ex-Sergeant Fulgencio Batista."

In March 1958, Pedro Miret landed a small plane on a strip in the Sierra Maestra—the first rebel airport. It was loaded with rifles, machine guns, mortar shells, and eighty thousand bullets. Fidel was now convinced that the M-26 could not lose. On March 12, he issued a manifesto asking Batista's army to rebel and the people to stop paying taxes to the government. "As from this instant," he said, "the country should consider itself in total war against the tyranny."

What Fidel was also banking on was the success of a general strike, secretly scheduled for April 9. But the strike was a total failure, mainly because the Communist unions refused to comply. Also, Batista's police were more brutal than ever. They killed five hundred people in Havana alone that day. By January 1, 1959, twenty thousand Cubans would die from police torture and executions.

The failure of the general strike demoralized the pro-M-26. Fidel reacted by talking on Radio Rebelde almost non-stop for the next week. He explained the situation, reminded people of Batista's crimes, described the guerrilla actions, outlined his program for the future, told the lives of those heroes fallen for the revolution—from Martí to Echevarría and Frank País. He so awakened the conscience of Cubans that Batista decided it was time to end the rebellion once and for all. He sent twelve thousand men, and an armada of modern tanks, cannons, armored cars, and planes loaded with napalm—all given him by the United States—against Fidel's three hundred weary guerrilleros.

7

"There was another side to the story," Che said when Batista's offensive began. "That was the half-heartedness with which Batista's army fought. Our boys fought like lions, one against ten or fifteen. Theirs surrendered quickly. After two and a half months of skirmishes, the enemy had one thousand casualties and had abandoned six hundred weapons. We handed four hundred and fifty prisoners to the Red Cross."

When Batista's offensive ended, Fidel immediately ordered the barbudos to come down from the Sierra and launch the counterattack. Che and Camilo Cienfuegos, who now headed Column Three, were told to head for Las Villas, in the center of the island, to join the Faure Chomón's rebels there—and cut Cuba in two.

Just as they began, on September 1, 1958, a terrible cyclone struck the area the barbudos had to cross. It was hence impossible for them to travel by truck along back roads. Che has written about what an ordeal his men had to endure:

"From that moment on, we had to travel on horse-back or on foot. We were heavily loaded with ammunition, with a forty-rocket bazooka, and everything necessary for a long march . . .

"We had to cross rivers in flood, creeks, and brooks converted into rivers; we had to struggle unendingly to keep ammunition, guns, and rockets dry; we had to find fresh horses to replace the tired ones; we had increasingly to avoid populated areas as we moved beyond Oriente Province. We marched toilsomely through flooded terrain, attacked by hordes of mosquitoes which made rest stops unbearable. We ate little and badly, we drank water from streams that wound through the marshes, or even swamp water itself. We dragged ourselves along, in a pitiable state, during appalling days. We were quite enfeebled and furthermore lacked footwear; many comrades walked barefoot through the mud of southern Camaguey.

"During the night of September 9, our advance guard fell into an enemy ambush. Two courageous comrades met their death there. But the worst was that we were spotted by enemy forces who, from that moment on, harassed us without letup . . .

"One or two days later we arrived at Laguna Grande; at the same time Camilo and his column reached there, too. They were in better shape than we were. I remember the place well: It was absolutely infested by mosquitoes; it was impossible to get a moment's rest.

"Came days of grueling trudging across desolate stretches where we came upon nothing but water and mud. We suffered from thirst and hunger and we were scarcely able to move ahead. Our legs were like lead and our weapons weighed us down oppressively . . .

"In the midst of our troubles we never lacked for support from the peasants. There was always one to serve us as guide or keep us from starving . . .

"One afternoon we heard on our little field radio [of the] annihilation of the hordes led by Che Guevara. The news of our demise provoked delight among our little troop. However, little by little, they began to be attacked by pessimism: thirst, hunger, fatigue, a feeling of impotence in the face of the encircling enemy forces, and especially a terrible foot ailment, which made each step a torment, had transformed our group into an army of shadows. Day after day our physical condition deteriorated, and our meals—one day yes, another day no, the third day perhaps—were not such as to improve our condition. Our hardest days were those we spent under siege, near the Baraguá sugar mill, in pestilential swamps, without a drop of potable water, harassed by planes, without a single horse to aid the feebler among us to cross that unfriendly slough, our shoes completely rotted by this brackish, muddy water full of vegetation that lacerated our bare feet.

"When we broke through the encirclement of Baraguá, we were truly in a disastrous situation. We had no time to recover, because torrential downpours and the general inclemency of the weather, together with enemy attacks, obliged us to resume our march. The troops became more and more exhausted and disheartened.

"However, at the most critical moment, when insults, entreaties, and tongue lashings were the only way to get the weary men to advance, a distant vision sufficed to restore their courage and give new spirit to the group: a blue spot on the horizon toward the west, the blue of the Las Villas range, glimpsed for the first time by our men. From that moment on, privations were more bearable, everything seemed easier. We escaped the second ring of encirclement by swimming the Jucaro. We felt as if we had emerged from darkness.

"Two days later we were safe in the heart of the Trinidad-Sanctí Spíritus mountain range, ready to enter the new stage of the war."

The columns of Che and Camilo joined forces with Chomón's troops in the Trinidad section of the Escambray Mountains on October 6, 1958. They began to attack Batista's middle two days later. At the same time, Fidel launched an offensive in Oriente, aiming to seize Santiago. The combined rebel forces were now one thousand strong.

As Fidel's forces swept toward the city, volunteers popped up from every village. Soon his force numbered twenty-five hundred. Guarding Santiago were fifteen thousand Batistiano troops. But they had had enough.

Meanwhile, Che seized the major city of Santa Clara and began marching toward Havana. A huge armored train, loaded with new tanks, cannons, equipment of all types, given to Batista only a few days earlier by the United States Government, was sent to help the troops fighting Che. It was blown up by M-26 saboteurs.

Even this, and the fact that by now every journalist was reporting that 98 per cent of the Cuban people hated Batista, did not stop the United States from helping him. As late as December 12, 1958, U.S. Senator Allen J. Ellender said in Havana: "Is there a revolution here? I hadn't noticed any trouble." The U.S. army, naval, and air force missions continued to advise Batista's forces until the very end. And, U.S. aid kept filling his pockets.

But it didn't help his regime. By now Che and Camilo, striking in lightning-fast pincer sweeps, were wiping out the pockets of Batista troops which still tried to fight. Most of the soldiers simply dropped their guns and ran.

Finally, as the year ended, so did Batista's resistance. The garrison of Moncada Barracks, where the 26th of July Movement—and the Cuban Revolution—had begun, surrendered to Fidel without firing a shot. On January 1, 1959, General Fulgencio Batista fled to the Dominican Republic. The war was over.

8

Fidel was not interested in ruling the country. He had named Manuel Urrutia, one of the judges of the Moncada trial, as provisional president, and he let him handle business from the presidential palace. Instead, leaving Raúl in Santiago as commander of Oriente, he took his time coming up the eight hundred miles to Havana with one thousand men, stopping at every village on the way to talk to Cubans. Once in Havana, he was reunited with his son, Fidelito, and rode to the palace with the boy at his side. All he wanted was peace and justice. He hoped the new politicians, who had all been anti-Batista and were honest, could make sure Cubans got that.

But they couldn't. Obsessed with legalism, their only concern, it seemed, was to gain the respect of the major powers. They were especially anxious to please the United States.

And that, of course, was impossible. The United States Government had loved Batista, and so had most of American journalists. Except for a few, such as Herbert Matthews, they had rarely wandered out of Havana, had spent most of their worktime talking to U.S. Embassy or Batista officials and their playtime in the plush casinos, night clubs, and bars. They had rarely reported Batista's tortures, his massacres or, until the end, his corruption, and never told the story of the collusion of U.S. companies. When they went for a swim, they inevitably visited the fancy beach clubs, where blacks and the poor were forbidden entrance. Yet never did they even write that of all the miles of gorgeous white-sand beaches that surrounded Havana, only a stretch sixty feet long was open to the public at large.

And so now, after the Fidelista victory, they were eager to condemn the new regime. On January 2, 1959, the New York *Times* reported that already "every move on the island" was "under the [U.S.] Administration's best microscope for analysis." And a few days later, the United States dispatched three destroyers and two submarine tenders to Havana harbor, where they remained anchored.

To this, the government of President Urrutia and his Prime Minister Miró Cardona, both wealthy aristocrats, reacted by being still more servile to the U.S. Embassy. Understandably, the revolutionaries were getting irritated. They had not fought so long and so hard in order to have Batista's best ally tell them what to do, as if nothing had changed.

But, of course, it had. For one thing, Fidel, Raúl

and Juan Almeida were busy organizing the new army, and this army of young dedicated patriots was interested in only one thing: building a just Cuba. Part of that justice was to bring the Batista criminals to trial. Even before victory, Fidel had pleaded with the people through Radio Rebelde not to take justice into their own hands, not to revert to mob violence. He had promised that the guilty would be tried, and now he meant to keep his word.

But the United States, afraid that such trials would reveal American complicity, was against it. So, on February 13, Miró Cardona resigned. Fidel started looking for a new Prime Minister. But everywhere the people pressured him to take the job. He hated the idea. But finally he relented. He was sworn in on February 16. One of his first acts was to go ahead with the trials.

Since so many people wanted vengeance, so many had lost a dear one to Batista's butchers, Fidel decided to hold those trials in huge amphitheatres and carry them live on television. Only that way, he said, "could all those thousands of Cubans who thirst for revenge, who want to take a gun and go out on their own to get even, feel relief, and become peaceful again."

But the United States jumped at these trials to justify its hatred of an independent reformer. The U.S. press denounced the "carnival," condemned Fidel's "bloodthirstiness," and insisted to its Ameri-

can readers that this proved Fidel was a nasty man
—and should be overthrown.

Cubans reacted with anger. How dare the United
States continue to meddle in our affairs, they
said. By what right does the United States, which
was responsible for so much of our misery, pose as
our moral judge, they said. They staged a huge rally
in support of the trials. A million people showed up.
Among them were all the U.S. journalists then in
Havana. Fidel spoke, and at one point, he turned to
the journalists and said:

"Yes, gentlemen, we are determined to extermi-
nate the killers. They will not live on to murder again.
And you, ladies and gentlemen, where were your
voices when Batista was ruling here like Himmler's
Gestapo? Where? I didn't hear your voices when
they were torturing and murdering twenty thousand
of our finest sons and daughters. You were silent
then. And, yes, I will ask you again: Where were
your voices when the atomic bomb was dropped on
Hiroshima and Nagasaki, after the war was already
in the bag for the Allies? You were silent then.
Where were your voices when the innocent Americans Julius and Ethel Rosenberg were murdered?*

* Tried and condemned to death in 1952 for supposedly giving
atomic secrets to Russia, the Rosenbergs were executed in June
1953, despite the fact that the law under which they were tried
was applied retroactively, which has always been considered un-
constitutional, before and since, and that America's own atomic
scientists said that it was impossible for the Rosenbergs to have
done what they were supposed to.

An entire world outside your borders shouted its prayers and its outrage. Where were your voices then? What have you come to sit in judgment on? The execution of mankind's enemies—torturers, killers, war criminals. Did you not hold your Nuremberg trials? Why do you interfere with us when we try our mass killers?"

It had no effect. The United States Government and press condemned the trials and used them as a pretext to begin to foment a counterrevolution in Cuba. Batista's henchmen in exile in Miami were given money and weapons. CIA planes, piloted by Batista's Cuban exiles, began to raid the island. Saboteurs, trained and transported by the CIA, burned Cuban factories, sugar mills, and communication centers. A small undeclared war was on its way.

The trials themselves, meanwhile, went off without a hitch. Today, even the most anti-Castro critic admits that of the 550 Batista torturers and assassins found guilty and executed, not one was wrongly convicted. One eyewitness gave this report:

"There sat the defendant—former Captain Jesus Soto Blanco, of the old Cuban army. The bearded advocate general, the prosecuting attorney, read the indictment. On such and such a day the defendant had murdered, by firing squad, such and such a defendant. The total came to 110.

"Then the defendant came before the microphone. As he spoke you saw that the man was no fool; he went on to marshal his arguments with a considerable degree of skill, pleading that he was simply doing his duty as a Cuban patriot, acting as he had in what he regarded as the best interests of his country. He had only followed the orders of higher-ups; and in an army, and at war, any man who calls himself a man was obliged to do things, act in a way that violated his sense of humanity. As for himself, he had no regrets or apologies. What he had done he had done . . .

"Then the witnesses were called; they came singly to deliver their testimony. Each was a gaunt, earnest man or woman clearly of the countryside by their garb and their rustic manner.

"The first woman who spoke, a woman of fifty, told how the captain had come to their village, heading his detachment, took men at random from the homes, some fifteen of them, and shot them on the pavements outside their homes. She told the story with a wealth of plain, unvarnished, undramatic detail. I could see that even the correspondents were impressed.

"When she was asked to identify the captain who, she was informed, sat on the stage, she turned and scrutinized the faces of everybody near her. When her eyes came to the captain, she started. This was the first time she had seen him since the murder of her husband. She leaped from the microphone, her fingers clawed, rushing at him and screaming: 'Murderer, murderer! You murdered the father of my children!' . . .

"So witness after witness testified, and the women, always the women. One screamed as she recognized him, and was only prevented by the pleading of the guards from assaulting the Batista officer. Each time the crowds in the stands stirred uneasily; each time their voices went up as the women wept.

"The crowd could scarcely remain seated when a youngster of twelve told his story. 'My father was in the house,' he said, 'when the captain came in. He told my father to come with him. My father then took off his wrist watch and his ring and put them on my hand. I grabbed my father by the arm and tried to take him away from the officer.

"'The officer said, "Don't you worry, hombre, you'll get your father back right away." The captain told us all to lie down on the floor and not get up until the soldiers leave the village. But as soon as he took my father out, I got up from the floor and ran to the window. I saw the soldiers stand and aim and fire at my father and I saw him fall on the street.' The atmosphere had become unbearable as the witnesses testified, and this youngster was the climax . . ."

Such trials succeeded in maintaining order in face of the inflamed popular will. What would have happened was clearly illustrated in Manzavillo, when two defendants received only a twenty-five-year term instead of death. Riots broke out, then a general strike, and the two were almost lynched. No wonder that the Catholic journal *La Quincena* said: "When the world learns of the horrendous crimes under the Batista regime the executions of a few hundred guilty subjects will seem like a mild punishment."

But Americans did not learn. Instead, they heard that Fidel Castro bought oil from Russia; proof said the U.S. press that Fidel was a Communist. Of course, Fidel was no such thing, not yet. He knew Cuba needed oil yet couldn't waste good money for it. Russia offered Cuba oil in exchange for sugar. The United States wouldn't do a trade like that. So Fidel bought it from Russia.

But the United States Government told Texaco and Standard Oil, which had oil refineries in Cuba, not to refine the Russian crude oil. This was in violation of the agreement by which the refineries were contracted to always first refine oil for Cuba's needs. But now they refused. So Fidel took over the refineries. The United States reacted by cutting off Cuba's sugar quota, that agreement by which the United States promised to buy 700,000 tons of Cuban sugar at good prices every year. Without such sales, the Cuban economy would be in bad trouble. The United States predicted that Fidel would fall in just two months.

Instead, the vast majority of the Cubans worked even harder for the Revolution. By now Fidel and his revolutionaries were all working full time building a new Cuba. The army was constructing roads, putting up houses, schools, hospitals. Every army barracks on the island became a school. In the first thirty months, the Fidelistas built more classrooms

91

than previous governments had built in thirty years. Students from sixteen years and up were sent throughout the country to teach illiterate peasants how to read and write. They lived with the peasants, helped in the fields, then gave classes in the evening. Doctors and medical students were sent from Havana to help in the drive to wipe out disease. Within one year both illiteracy and that dreaded worm which infested young children were well on the way to being eradicated.

Electricity reached the backwoods, so did drinkable water. In a year, more than twenty-five thousand new homes were put up, replacing the old slums. The houses had three or four rooms, modern bathrooms, and good kitchens, even a garden. Recreation centers were opened up everywhere. The old country clubs were available to all. Rents were cut by 50 per cent. So was the cost of electricity, and when the owners (the U.S. companies) refused to lower their rates, they were taken over, nationalized, by the government.

Every adult was guaranteed a job. New universities were launched. Fisheries were started, and twenty new ships were put into the water by the end of 1960. Wherever help was needed, there came the barbudos. In fact, they were so busy doing constructive things, there was no one available to be a cop. So, boy scouts directed traffic in the daytime and office workers volunteered to do it at night. And robberies? Crimes? There were none.

The Fidelistas did create a militia. Made up of man and women who had regular jobs, the militia were trained at lunchtime and weekends. Their members learned to handle weapons. Their task was to defend the island from invaders, and everyone was beginning to expect those invaders to come from America.

Nevertheless, as late as September 1960, when Fidel came to New York to speak at the United Nations, he hoped good relations could be established between America and Cuba—as equals. Cuba needed aid. But the kind he was offered, no self-respecting patriot could accept. "We'll give you all the aid you need," said Christian Herter, then President Eisenhower's Secretary of State, "on one condition: You absolutely guarantee all U.S. interests in Cuba." That meant American companies could continue to exploit Cubans, take their profits out of the country; in one phrase, keep Cuba poor.

Said Fidel: "Go to hell!"

9

Fidel knew that from then on his economy was going to get rougher and rougher. After all, 60 per cent of everything in Cuba was American—cars, machines, telephones, bicycles, watches, even lipsticks. From then on it would be impossible to fix many of these things when they broke. Shortages would get worse and worse. And in order to get money to buy important things, Cubans would have to export all they could but import as little as possible. That meant that there would even be food shortages. Cubans would have to go without cigars, which was one of their great industries, and without meat. Cubans would even have to eat less sugar so it could be sold in Europe in exchange for necessary machines to build the island into a modern country. Yes, life was not going to be easy.

But most Cubans accepted that fate with renewed energy. Instead of falling, Fidel's government became more and more popular. Its agrarian reform, which took away the land from the rich and gave it, under government supervision, to the poor, was a tremendous success. All exploiters lost their land. No one could bribe or plead exception, not even Fidel's mother. She had taken over Angel Castro's plantation when he had died in 1956 and was running it with Fidel's oldest brother, Ramón. Their land was the first to be nationalized. Fidel's mother was outraged and turned against her son (though not Ramón, who remained a Fidelista). Fidel ordered the land turned over to the guajiros who worked it, on a collective basis.

It was the same everywhere. Now the guajiros became state employees. They had guaranteed incomes. They no longer had to travel from town to town looking for work. They had homes, civic centers, schools, a new life. If the U.S. press scoffed because they rarely ate meat, the guajiros laughed in turn. They had never had meat before, and now they at least had as much as anyone else.

The Fidelistas also eliminated exploitation in the cities. They confiscated the luxury hotels, owned by Batistianos or American gangsters, and turned them into boarding schools. They opened government stores everywhere and sold goods cheaper. They weeded out all speculators. And they let anyone who was not a criminal leave. Never before in the history of the world has a revolutionary government allowed all its opponents to leave the country freely. In Cuba, it meant that most of the rich left, and since the rich were the educated, it hurt Cuba because it lost its technicians, its doctors, its dentists. But, said Fidel, "I'd rather these people leave than work here against their will. We will train our own technicians." And they did. Within three years, Cuba had more and better doctors than ever before. What's more, these doctors were young, enthusiastic, and proud. They weren't interested in money but in helping Cuba and the revolution. They were willing, in fact, anxious to work in the most remote corners of the island, places where people had never seen a doctor before.

The more the United States made difficulties for Fidel, the more Cubans loved him. And he was always available to any Cuban, even just to talk. He traveled everywhere, sometimes driving his own jeep alone. He stopped on any excuse, often to give a lift to some hitchhiker and would immediately engage him in a heated conversation about Cuba. The French writer Jean-Paul Sartre once spent a couple of days with Fidel on the road. Sartre was struck by his simplicity:

"He was about to continue when we were stopped. This time by a single Negro, gigantic and furious. He came from behind a wall, as we were going through a little town with low houses, and threw himself at us. With the flat of his hand, he violently pounded the hood.

"'You rash fool!' he told Fidel with anger. 'Protect your life. It belongs to us, not to you! What are you doing in the front of this car? You know damn well that they can shoot at you from above, that you can crash into a truck. What would we do, huh? We would look fine. Go sit in the back with Celia and do me the favor of seating all these people who are lounging in the rear in the front.'

"'They are my guests,' said Fidel with a smile.

"The Negro shrugged his shoulders. 'So what? Drive them around as much as you want, but if someone has to die, it might as well be them . . .'

"Fidel smiled broadly; the Negro returned his smile, but shook his finger at him . . .

"The automobile was stopped ten more times. It was like an omnibus. We picked up an old peasant woman who was waiting for her bus and dropped her off in front of her village."

Later they arrived at Fidel's home, where they were to spend the night.

"I entered," Sartre continued. "It was a barracks room. On either side of the central corridor were bedsteads, double-deckers. There were about twenty mattresses, and on each one a cover. I did not immediately understand, I admit, that the head of the government, his brother, his family, and his guests would spend the night in this dormitory."

Part of Fidel's popularity came, of course, from just this, his simplicity. The people of Cuba knew he was genuinely one of theirs. He lived much like they did, talked the same language, ate the same food—often with them—and enjoyed the same fun. Seeing kids play baseball or basketball as he would drive by, for example, he would invariably stop, get out, and join them for an hour or so. He knew how to listen and certainly knew how to talk. Oh, how he could talk. For hours and hours he would explain everything and anything, from the most complicated problem of the economy to what his own doubts were all about. He'd visit farms and work in the fields. He'd inspect a factory and join the production line. And it wasn't just a show. The people sensed he was really concerned. He wanted to know how things worked and how people felt working there. He wanted to learn from the people, and he wanted to tell them what he had learned. Cubans adored him.

Not all, to be sure. When Fidel ordered the land reform, landowners went on the radio in Pinar del Rio and denounced him every fifteen minutes. They called him a thief, a rat and, worst of all in their eyes, a Communist.

DO NOT TRY TO CONVINCE ME THAT THE
    CUBAN REVOLUTION IS COMMUNIST!
BECAUSE IF YOU CONVINCE ME . . .
    I WILL BECOME A COMMUNIST!

read a sign on a door in Sanctí Spíritus. But the United States Government refused to hear the truth. To the Republican Party in power (as well as to the Democrats who coveted that power) anyone who touched private property was a Communist. And if that property was owned by Americans, my God!

It didn't matter if the Americans in question were responsible for people starving to death, anyone touching them must be exterminated.

At the beginning, some U.S. journalists tried to make a difference between Che Guevara and Fidel. It was Che, who was now running the state bank, who was the real Red, they said. Fidel, they thought, was wavering. This led one revolutionary in Cuba to tell the following joke.

"Somehow the Fidelistas have been beaten and they are being punished by being buried in mud, the depth of which is determined by how Communistic they were. Juan Almeida, head of the rebel army, is in mud up to his ankles. President Dorticós [who replaced Urrutia] is up to his waist. Fidel is in mud up to his neck. He looks around and sees Raúl only up to his knees. 'Eh Raúl,' Fidel shouts, 'how come you're only up to your knees?' Raúl puts his finger to his lips and says, 'Shhh, I'm standing on Che's shoulders.'"

The fact is that Fidel, Che, Raúl, all of Cuba's revolutionaries were neither red nor black but genuine revolutionaries. They wanted to establish a country where no one was exploited, where everyone had the same opportunity, where everyone, regardless of race or color or family income, had the best possible education, and where medical services, dentistry, education, recreational services, all the necessities of life were free. Those who made personal fortunes from these necessities, who preferred to see peasants starve, children die of worm infestations, and the vast majority of the people be miserable just so they could have a life of luxury, obviously became enemies to the Fidelistas. Most of those rich were Americans, or Cubans who worked with Americans. Those same rich Americans gave money both to the Republican and Democratic parties, both of whom in turn supported the rich. Because the press, television, radio, advertising cost so much money, few politicians can become well known and get elected unless they have money to advertise. So, most of those who *do* get elected owe their first allegiance not to the country, not to those who vote for them, but to the rich who give them money. It follows that, under the present system, any American President is likely to be against those who believe in real equality. Thus the United States Government was pro-Batista and anti-Fidel. It actively tried to undermine the Fidelista government right from the start.

Fidel knew that eventually the United States would invade Cuba. To defend his country he tried to get arms. Not from Russia or Communist countries, but from anyone who wanted to sell to Cuba. He got some arms from the Belgians. They were loaded on a French ship, *La Coubre,* and brought to Havana. As they were being unloaded, on March 4, 1960, a terrific explosion rocked the city: CIA agents had bombed the ship. Some seventy-five people were killed and three hundred injured.

But this was only the beginning. Before leaving office, President Eisenhower had ordered that bases be set up to train and launch an invasion army against Cuba. That order was given, Ike admitted later, on March 17, 1960; two months later, a Princeton opinion institute reported that 86 per cent of the Cuban people were enthusiastic supporters of Fidel. Nevertheless, President Kennedy, after his inauguration, did not change that order. On the contrary, he allotted more money and more experts to the task.

The U.S. press, meanwhile, was on an anti-Castro rampage. In July, *Life* ran a screaming headline on "Police State Tactics in Castro's Cuba" (though the story itself contradicted the headline). The San Francisco *Examiner*, which had already called Fidel "a lunatic with a Hitlerian complex who follows the Communist line" in an editorial, now ran a cartoon called "Blood Brothers," showing a fat and sinister Mao grasping Fidel's hands; both their hands were dripping with blood. The San Francisco *Chronicle* talked of a "love rite" between Russia's Nikita Khrushchev and Fidel.

During the 1960 election campaigns, Kennedy desperately tried to outvoice Richard Nixon, the Republican candidate, on a let's-be-tough-on-Castro policy. He openly talked of a U.S.-backed invasion. In October, Eisenhower put an embargo on trade with Cuba, meaning that anyone who wanted to trade with the United States must not trade with Cuba.

In November, all Batista-exile forces were grouped together (by the CIA) into one "front." The front was armed, and its agents were parachuted or speed-boated into Cuba. They set off bombs wherever they could, burned sugar crops, killed Cuban militiamen. The tactic was to bring the Cuban economy to a halt before the spring sugar harvest. Then, an invasion of twenty-nine mercenaries, including three CIA agents, were sent in from Florida. Their aim was to start a guerrilla base in the Escambray Mountains; they were caught and the three Americans were executed. Finally, on November 18, Eisenhower sent planes and battleships to Guatemala and Nicaragua, whose dictators were second only to Batista in torture and corruption, supposedly at their requests. The invasion was being readied.

For the next few months, not a day passed without some terrorist activity in Cuba. Light planes, supposedly owned by private Cuban exiles but actually flown by CIA pilots, dropped bombs on various Cuban towns, including Havana. On January 2, 1961, while Fidel was speaking at a rally commemorating the second anniversary of his victory, a bomb exploded in Havana. "It is the U.S. which is paying the terrorists," explained Fidel. The next day, just days before Kennedy's inauguration, Eisenhower broke off diplomatic relations with Cuba, saying,

"Our sympathy goes out to the people of Cuba."

On February 27, 1961, the *Journal* reported: "It's no secret that this country is already furnishing weapons and supplies to anti-Castro forces in central Cuba's Escambray Mountains and training counter-revolutionaries in Florida and Guatemala."

But no one in the U.S. press criticized the planned invasion. Not one official even wondered out loud if it was in the American people's interest for tax money to be used to pay high salaries to former Batista criminals, torturers, and exploiters, to train them, arm them, and transport them to overthrow the only popular government Cuba had ever had.

In Cuba, all this terror and preparation had its unfortunate toll. Instead of using its precious resources to build up the country's economy, Fidel had to shift them to defense. More militiamen had to be trained and armed. A secret police to track down terrorists and saboteurs had to be created; Ramiro Valdés, Fidel's Interior Minister, brilliantly whipped one up in a hurry. The trouble is that when one is threatened on every side by armed thugs it becomes very difficult to differentiate between dissenters and enemies; thus, the secret police began to round up innocent opponents as well as saboteurs, and Cuba lost some of its freedom.

The invasion finally came off April 16 and 17, 1961. In the weeks before, President Kennedy had desperately tried to get approval of U.S. action from other Latin-American nations. Despite the fact that all of them are tied to U.S. companies, importers and exporters, and government aid, only the hard-line dictators gave him solid approval. As a result, Kennedy decided to give the invasion force limited support. He ordered the CIA to bombard Cuban airports on April 16, but canceled further raids.

On April 17, the main body of the invasion army —some 1,300 men, equipped with tanks, cannons, bazookas, heavy machine guns, mortars, and the best of U.S. small arms, and transported in U.S. landing barges—landed on a small beach in an enclave on the central Cuban coast known, only too appropriately, as the Bay of Pigs. The local militia immediately sprang into action, holding off the elite corps for a whole day with meager weapons. That gave time for Fidel's airplanes to sink the invader's ships, eliminating retreat, and for his army, which he led himself, to encircle the beachhead. On the second day, after 90 of their forces had been killed, the remaining 1,214 invaders surrendered.

Cuba's victory was total. The next day, people put up huge signs all over Havana. They read: "If Americans don't want to live with a socialist revolution 90 miles from their shores, they'd better move."

10

President Kennedy had said: "The test was whether the Cuban people would back a revolt against Castro." They didn't. Not only that, they mobilized so enthusiastically that it seemed every Cuban was willing to die to save their government, their independence, and their honor. In fact, that is exactly how they felt.

Of American newsmen, Herbert Matthews of the New York *Times*, best understood what happened:

"One of the many miscalculations made by the Americans was to underrate Fidel Castro, his followers, and the strength of the popular following he had among the Cuban people.

"Military technicians in the United States went on speculating about what would have happened if President Kennedy had not canceled the second air strike, or if he had allowed the American Marines and pilots to do more than they did. But this was typical military nonsense.

"It was exactly the type of mechanical thinking

that led the United States deeper and deeper into the quicksand of the Vietnamese war. On paper, in the Pentagon, North Vietnam and the Vietcong should have been defeated once the Americans put their immensely superior power and wealth into the conflict. However, the Vietnamese had something that military minds find it impossible to gauge—spirit. They fought for their country, their race, their traditions, their freedom as they saw it, their dignity as human beings having a right to settle their own affairs . . .

"The same thing happened in Cuba at the time of the Bay of Pigs invasion. It would have happened later if the missile crisis had led to armed conflict. It will happen again if the United States, for any reason, leads another 'crusade' against communism in Cuba or against the Castro regime, or against any regime that had been chosen and set up by Cubans themselves.

"The folly of the American government in believing that 1,400 Cuban exiles, armed, trained, supported and guided by the United States, could have held a beachhead in Cuba against the Castro forces was beyond belief at the time . . ."

Cuban patrols spotted the invasion almost at once. Its planes reacted quickly and surely. The militia fought hard and well. All troops stayed loyal. And, as Arthur Schlesinger, Jr., who advised Kennedy on both Cuba and Vietnam, and became an opponent to the Vietnam war only when it was fashionable to do so, said at the time: "Fidel never panicked, and if faults were chargeable to him they were his over-estimate of the strength of the invasion and undue caution in pressing the ground attack against the beachhead. His performance was impressive."

Added Matthews: "Fidel Castro is always at his best in moments of crisis. This is one of the keys to his hold over the Cuban people, and it will be one of his claims to an outstanding position in the history of our times."

For a while it was thought in Cuba that the danger was over. Restrictions were dropped. People began to talk freely again. And the government, wanting to return to the task of building the country, asked all Cubans to let bygones be bygones. Fidel even went on TV with the captured invaders to discuss the future with them.

It was an amazing performance: Fidel taking time to explain to those who had come to kill him and destroy the revolution what the revolution was all about. Some of the prisoners argued. Others asked questions. Twice they applauded him. At one point, after pointing out that they were used by U.S. interests, Fidel asked if they would be on Cuba's side if the United States made a direct attack on Cuba.

"Would the people permit us to bear arms, to defend Cuba in such an event?" one of the prisoners asked.

"Your case is difficult," Fidel said. "It is difficult for the people to understand why severe penalties should not be applied. There is horror over those who have fallen; there are many orphans, there is hatred. I have not invented these feelings."

Then Fidel turned to the militiamen guarding the prisoners and asked them "as a part of the people, what should be done with the prisoners?"

"*Paredón!*" they shouted in unison, meaning the execution wall.

Fidel shook his head. Mass executions would "sully the Revolution," he said. Then, to the captives, he promised he would try to convince Cubans to find a more humane solution. (Eventually, in mid-1963, the prisoners were returned to the United States in exchange for $57 million worth of food and medicine.) A few days later, at a rally on May 1, 1961, Fidel begged Cubans to be generous. "This is the hour in which we, far from using the moment against those who do not understand, should ask them if the time has not come for them to join us. The Revolution does not want to use force against a minority. The Revolution wants all Cubans to understand."

But Kennedy refused to understand—or to seek peace. Instead, three days later, on May 4, it was reported from Washington that at a meeting with Cuban exiles his "offers of co-operation were definite and his backing was total and absolute."

Fidel had no choice. He now had to arm Cuba for another attack, more serious this time. He asked for Russian help.

As Russian arms arrived in Cuba, Kennedy panicked. In September, he asked Congress for authority to call up 150,000 reserves in the event of an emergency. And he complained at the United Nations. "Were the United States able to give Cuba effective guarantees concerning the integrity of Cuban territory," the Cuban ambassador answered, "then Cuba would not have to strengthen its defenses, Cuba would not even need an army, and all resources that are used for this could be gratefully and happily invested in the economic and cultural development of the country."

America was deaf. Kennedy ordered the island put under surveillance. On September 21, *Time* magazine called for "a direct U.S. invasion with sufficient force to get the job done with surgical speed and efficiency." On October 10, Senator Keating of New York said he had proof that intermediate-range missile sites were under construction in Cuba. On October 22, Kennedy, on a nationwide TV address, informed the world he was setting up a "quarantine" around Cuba. It meant a blockade, which has always been interpreted in law and history as an act of war. The world had come to the edge of destruction.

But Russia gave in. It promised to withdraw its missiles if the United States gave its word not to invade Cuba. The United States accepted on condition that it could send agents all over Cuba to check. Fidel refused. Russia took out its missiles anyway, and American spy planes verified all were gone. But Kennedy refused to issue a no-invasion promise.

The United States won the missile crisis. But to the rest of the world it lost its honor. Never again would a small country trust the United States. Everywhere in the poor world, in Asia, Africa, and Latin America, people felt that it was the United States which was trying to dominate the world. It was the United States that would risk war and total destruction to force small countries to have the kind of government it wanted.

Patriots and nationalists in small countries stopped seeking help from the United States. Instead they turned toward Russia, toward China, but mostly toward each other. Cuba, Algeria, Vietnam, Korea became the center of the revolutionary world, of the new world. And as the Vietnamese became the most striking example of the poor people's rebellion against the American economic dictatorship, it was clear that the process which would end the American empire had begun.

Fidel himself expressed this sentiment well in speeches and talks during the next few years:

"In the United States, many people proclaim that they are defending liberty in other countries. But what kind of liberty is it that they are defending, that nobody is grateful to them, that nobody appreciates this alleged defense of their liberties? What has happened in Korea, in Formosa, in South Vietnam? What country has prospered and has achieved peace and political stability under that protection from the United States? What solutions has it found to the great problems of the world? . . .

"Look at the case of Cuba: The United States wants to 'liberate' Cuba from communism, but in reality Cuba doesn't want to be 'liberated' from communism. In order to 'liberate' Cuba from communism, the United States organized the followers of Batista, the most reactionary people of this country —torturers, conspirators, exploiters of all types, thieves. It organized them, trained them, and armed them in order to come to 'liberate' the people of Cuba. None of those people had solved the problem of unemployment, ignorance, lack of medical care, the poverty and misery that existed in this country before the Revolution.

"Tell me, for what purpose did the United States come to 'liberate' us at the Bay of Pigs? To re-establish the power of the landowners, of the managers of its monopolistic businesses, of thieves, or torturers? In what sense can that be called liberty? . . .

"It would be ridiculous if we were to say to Americans: 'If you want to do business and have good relations with us, give up your bourgeois ideas,' and if we were to impose conditions on what they were allowed to do in their country. It would be so ridiculous that it wouldn't occur to anybody. OK, well neither should it occur to them to tell us what to do, because that is also utterly ridiculous. They talk of Marxism, about not being able to tolerate it, about

111

not being able to allow it. And who are they to say how each country should be governed? Who are they to dictate laws behind the frontiers of other countries? Our right, like the right of any country in Latin America, is and must always be to choose the system of government which we consider suitable. If any country doesn't want a revolution, they shouldn't make one. That's a matter for the country to decide. And if they want one, they should make one. It's every country's right to decide . . .

"The presence of the Cuban Revolution, alarming the imperialists and keeping them awake at night, is one of the best things that could happen to the other countries of Latin America, even though there hasn't been a revolution there [since the Cuban Revolution].

"If the Yankee imperialists take the liberty of bombing wherever they please and of sending mercenary troops to repress the revolutionary movement in any part of the world, the revolutionary peoples have the right to help, including by their physical presence, any people fighting against the Yankee imperialists.

"In Latin America, there should never be one, or two, or three peoples fighting alone against imperialism. The correlation of imperialist forces to those of this continent, the proximity of their home territory, the energy with which they would try to defend their domains in this part of the world, demands on this continent more than in any other part of the world a common strategy, a common, simultaneous battle.

"Unfortunately, Cuba's forces are limited. But within the limits of these forces, in the best manner possible, and in the most decided manner and the most appropriate according to the circumstances, the Cuban Revolution offers and will give its maximum support.

"We are a small country, very close to the coasts of the imperialist metropolis; our armaments are chiefly defensive weapons; but our men, our revolutionary militants, our fighters are ready to fight with all their might against the imperialists in any part of the world . . ."

11

Fidel was very serious. Cubans began to train revolutionaries from Africa, Asia, and Latin America. They sent volunteers to fight oppression in Portuguese Guinea, the Congo, Colombia, Guatemala, Venezuela, and the Cameroons. They sent arms, food, technicians to North Vietnam and to almost every revolutionary group in the poor countries. In 1966, they invited representatives from all these groups to a solidarity conference in Havana—known as the Tri-Continental meeting. And in 1967, they brought together in their capital guerrilla fighters from all over Latin America.

Their aim was not just to talk, but to act. Cubans proposed mutual assistance agreements, real material help, mutual communications systems, and co-ordination of all their activity.

Those who claimed that Cuba was a satellite of the Soviet Union, as did the U.S. press, for example, were blind to reality. The reality was that after the 1962 missile crisis Russia felt defeated. It wanted no confrontation with the United States. It considered the United States something of a rabid dog, willing to bite anyone who stood up to it, and it had no intention of being bitten. Russia claimed it wanted peace, nothing but peace, and it was willing to suffer any American insult not to provoke U.S. anger.

This policy of appeasement Russia called "peaceful coexistence." Under it, Russia helped the North Vietnamese very little. While the United States poured billions of dollars' worth of arms and half a million men to sustain one corrupt and brutal military dictatorship after another in South Vietnam, Russia sent the North some token planes, a few outdated anti-aircraft missiles, and boxes of candy. (Though the Soviets did increase their aid when the United States Air Force began blanketing Vietnam with so many bombs that each week more destructive tonnage was dropped on that poor and tiny country than had been dropped on Germany during the whole of World War II.)

Toward Cuba, Russia's policy was the same. It disapproved of its revolutionary fervor, used every economic pressure it could to force Fidel to keep its volunteers home. In 1965, Che Guevara and other revolutionary leaders went to fight for Congolese independence. Russia was furious. It threatened reprisals against Cuba. Fidel had no choice: he called back his men, though by then three barbudos had died there.

It's not that Fidel and the Cuban revolutionaries were not Communists. They did so consider themselves. None of the barbudos had been Communists when they were fighting in the Sierra Maestra. All of them became Communists gradually, as they learned that what the word really means is wanting to share everything together. When they realized that poverty, exploitation, disease, illiteracy, unemployment, and misery can only be exterminated when all men work together for the common good and share together in common, or *in commune*, the fruits of their labor, then, and only then, did they declare themselves Communists.

But they were not the Russian type of Communists. They did not believe in only helping themselves at the expense of others who are called allies. No, they believed that no man is free until all men are free. Or as their hero, José Martí, put it: "As long as there is one man who sleeps in the mud, there should not be another who sleeps in a bed of gold."

Cuba is governed by a party. It is called the Communist Party. Like any other such organization, in Russia or Europe or America, it has a Central Committee which is elected by the party members. It also has a Political Bureau, which decides the basic lines that the government should take. Fidel, Raúl, Almeida, Valdés, Dorticós, and many of the original M-26 fighters are on the Central Committee. Some of these are also in the Political Bureau. But not one member of the bureau belonged to Cuba's old Communist Party, that group which obeyed the policies of Moscow. In fact, many of the old Communist Party were kicked out of Cuba by Fidel, and some were even jailed for a while.

In fact, however, it is Fidel who rules Cuba. But in no way does that mean he is the kind of dictator which the American press pretends he is. Or else his form of dictatorship is one of the most democratic ever devised. It is a constant dialogue between him and the people. There are very few Cubans who have not seen Fidel in the flesh, argued with him, shared a meal with him. As Herbert Matthews of the New York *Times* said: "Watching Fidel mingling with and talking to workers and peasants is impressive—how natural they are with him, how lacking in any servility, and how simply he talks to them, without any sense of superiority, condescension, or the slightest arrogance."

Fidel calls contact with the people his second university: he learns from them the real problems of everyday life—and he can only keep their confidence because he does something about those problems. "The reactionaries mistrust mankind," he said. "They think that a human being is still something of a beast—that he only moves under the lash of a whip. They think he can be motivated only by selfish interest. The revolutionary believes in man; he believes in the human race. If one does not believe in a human being, then one is not a revolutionary."

But communication, trust, genuine dedication to revolution are not always enough. Sooner or later, results matter. And if there are no results, people become demoralized. And then apathy sets in.

For years Cuban youth, which is the backbone of the Revolution, willingly endured hardships and overwork for the cause. The young knew that a great deal of Cuba's resources were going to help other revolutionaries. And they were proud to go by the thousands to plant coffee beans, cut sugar, build dams during long hours. It was their way of being with Che, fighting elsewhere in the poor world.

Che had been pulled out of the Congo on Russian orders. The Russians could back such orders with economic blackmail. Dependent on oil for its factories, its electric power, and its agricultural revolution, Cuba needed Russian oil to keep going. But Russia did not want Che or any other Cuban stirring up trouble in Africa. Fidel could have reacted by telling the Russians to go to hell. After all, that's what he had said to the United States. But there was a marked difference between the strings attached to U.S. and Russian aid. The United States wanted to run the *inside* of the country and wanted to take profits *out* of the country. In effect, the more aid a country gets from the United States the poorer it becomes, and the worse off are its common folk.

The Russians, on the other hand, made no such conditions. Yes, they wanted the recipient country to vote with them in the United Nations, and in the case of Cuba, Soviet aid meant that Fidel had to stop helping African revolutionaries. But Russian aid did help Cubans. It built factories, developed new agricultural lands, put up fisheries, constructed whole new ports, and gave Cubans the arms with which to defend themselves. Russia did not meddle in the domestic affairs of Cuba. It did not take profits out of the country. Only if a country is actually next door to Russia, does it risk Russian interference or even outright intervention, as in the case of Czechoslovakia.

But still Fidel was angry. He was willing to order Che and other Cubans out of the Congo, but not willing to accept Russia's "peaceful coexistence" line. That line, he said, only allows America to invade more countries—like Vietnam—without a Russian response. Fidel wanted to help revolutionaries, not only out of solidarity and a moral commitment to justice, but also out of self-defense. The more revolutionaries confront the American attempt to impose its form of democracy (meaning control by the rich), the less chance there is for a U.S. invasion of Cuba.

Russia and Cuba worked out a compromise. If Fidel kept his revolutionaries out of Asia and Africa he was free to do as he pleased in Latin America. And so Che went to Bolivia.

Armed rebellion failed in Bolivia for various reasons. First, because the revolutionaries who went there—Cubans, Peruvians, Argentines, Chileans—and the Bolivians who joined them did not know the area well enough. Second, because they did not speak the dialects of the local peasants and could not establish good contact with them, and thus could not get their support. Third, because the United States was ready for them; CIA agents had long reconnoitered the area and its anti-guerrilla specialists, using planes equipped with very sensitive heat spotters which could track any moving object, were quickly on top of them. Fourth, because, unlike Cuba where the history of the M-26 dating back to the Moncada attack was well known by the people, no psychological, political, or propaganda campaigns preceded the rebellion; people barely knew of its existence and had no way of having faith in it. Fifth, because the local Communist Party, which controlled Bolivia's underground communications, refused to help. Sixth, and most crucial, because Bolivians are not Cubans, and what worked in Cuba did not necessarily work elsewhere.

That last point, in fact, was the hardest but most important lesson Cuba learned from the Bolivia defeat. Che was killed in October 1967, but the lesson didn't strike Fidel for a whole year. But then he understood: Cubans had accomplished the revolution in Cuba. Bolivians would do it in Bolivia—their way. Maybe their way would be different. Maybe Bolivian miners would succeed in rushing their presidential palace; they had tried and failed in the past, maybe that was their Moncada.

Every poor country of the world is going to rebel in

the decades to come. Every one is going to throw out its exploiters and corrupt politicians. But each one is going to do it in keeping with its history and culture and tradition. In Argentina, where unions are big and tough, the revolution will probably be led by urban workers. In Peru, where the army has rarely been corrupt and usually been proudly nationalistic, revolutionary generals have already put into effect an agrarian reform almost as sweeping and important as Cuba's. In Chile, where elected governments usually finished their terms without interference from would-be military dictators, the revolution might be accomplished by an elected president and his party. Already, Socialist President Salvador Allende has kicked most unscrupulous American companies out of the country and nationalized the country's basic resources.

When Fidel learned his lesson, he called home his fighters. "Let's develop this country," he told them, "let's make Cuba strong, self-sufficient, fully educated, modern. And if any revolutionary asks for help we'll give it to him. But let him do his revolution, like we did, like the Chinese, the Algerians, and, for twenty-five years against incredible odds, the Vietnamese." Uruguay's Tupamaros, the armed forces of the country's National Liberation Movement, did ask Fidel for money and arms. He gave it to them—until they learned to win their own in battle. Then he stopped.

12

The death of Che and the failure of the Bolivian rebellion were hard blows for Cubans. Harder still, though, was going to be their economy, unless something was done about it fast. It had begun deteriorating on all sides.

Fidel had pushed the social benefits of the revolution too far too fast. By 1968, public telephones, transportation, all sporting events, recreation facilities, movies, medicine, eyeglasses, schooling, nurseries, school meals, milk for children, textbooks were free. Rent was 10 per cent of the family income, unless the family had lived in the apartment or house for ten years or more. In that case it was free, more important, it then belonged to the family. The poor paid almost nothing for their light and stove, but those richer people who had remained in Cuba in big houses and were using power to run appliances, television sets, and big freezers were paying more.

There were almost 400,000 *becados* by then, boys and girls from the country living as boarders in fancy Vedado homes abandoned by the rich who had fled to Miami. The becados received not only their housing and food, but clothes, books, transportation home on weekends all free, plus a small monthly allowance.

The Revolution had pushed nonconformity hard too. Students were goaded into questioning everything. They didn't like the official newspaper, they seized a printing press and put out their own: *Juventud Rebelde* (Rebellious Youth). They didn't like an official text, they wrote their own. Students ran schools, television programs, a radio station, and the official book publication center. They published everything of interest, from Manchester's puff-job book on the Kennedys to the work of Trotsky, banned in Russian-type Communist countries.

The courts, also, were revolutionized. Most were simply disbanded. Now local neighborhoods elected a "judge." He was given a quick course and told to keep his regular job. As one explained: "All cases are held at times when the whole neighborhood can come; it's like a community debate. But the object is not to punish or jail anyone anyway, for we are going to do away with jails." And they did too. Even the Isle of Pines Presidio, where revolutionaries used to be jailed and where Fidelistas at first kept the saboteurs and counterrevolutionaries, was destroyed—except for the one cell where Fidel served his Moncada time; that was maintained as a museum. The Isle of Pines became the Isle of Youth, run by the young (maximum age: twenty-seven) as an agri-cultural center.

Even traditional taboos for women were attacked. First, girls were encouraged to become independent, go to school, learn a trade. By 1968, 48 per cent of the new doctors were women. Next, women were put into managerial and responsible posts, stimulat-ing others to follow their independent road. Cuban men, even revolutionaries, used to the "macho" Latin cult whereby a woman only takes care of the house, works as a servant or secretary, fought hard against the "new" womanhood.

Contradictions arose. In Havana's special school to train women for directing traffic, trainees learned to handle guns and judo for self-defense in the morn-ings, how to apply make-up in the afternoons. But schools were kept segregated by sexes. Marriages were threatened. One woman, who signed up for a two-year stretch on the Isle of Youth, was told by her husband he'd divorce her if she went. She went. He divorced her.

Nevertheless, the Fidelistas tried. *Granma*, the of-ficial newspaper, editorialized: "The incorporation of women into work is not exclusively a question of the need for increasing our labor force. More im-portant is the need for building a society in which everyone is a worker, everyone a soldier, everyone a student. This implies, as a matter of principle, the complete social liberation of women."

All of these measures, reforms, and constructions

cost money, a great deal of it. Cuba didn't have money; it had sugar. But the upheaval in the new society hurt production. Also raw materials and machinery parts no longer came from the United States in the constant flow that the ferryboat from Florida had made possible. Now ships had to bring the stuff from as far as Russia and China. That meant big docks had to be built, and long-range planning was needed. But no one knew how to plan for breakdowns and shortages in advance. By 1962, meat, milk, shoes, and soap had to be rationed.

Making Cuba self-sufficient meant diversifying agriculture. But sugar lands could not be eliminated since sugar was still the cheapest product to grow in Cuba that would bring in the most needed cash. So new lands had to be cleared. But that, in turn, required heavy bulldozers, which Cuba didn't have. So, at first, Cuba planted rice, tomatoes, citrus fruits, vegetables on sugar land, thus cutting down its buying power, which meant it still could not get those bulldozers. The population as a whole ate better, but long-term progress was not yet established.

And all that construction! The Fidelistas built thousands of homes in the first years. That pleased the people, and God knows they needed homes. But had the material been used to build factories, in the long run the pay-off would have been surer. The worse the economy became, the more Fidel called for sacrifice. For a while people responded. But then they began to feel discouraged.

In October 1963, the longest and hardest hurricane ever to hit Cuba smashed the eastern part of the island. Hundreds died, over a million head of cattle drowned, Cuba's entire coffee crop was lost. Fidel reacted with vigor. He was everywhere, helping, comforting, giving directions—and almost got drowned himself. He ordered all Cubans to share the hurricane's cost equally, and asked for thousands of volunteers to help rebuild the area. Cubans responded, and the volunteer system carried on after the emergency. From then on, every able-bodied Cuban, from Fidel himself, Dorticós, all cabinet members down to office employees, bus drivers, and students, spent weeks, sometimes months, in volunteer agricultural work.

The economy picked up somewhat. By 1967, Cuba was exporting meat, fruits, coffee, and leather goods in addition to sugar and cigars. But the shortages were just as great and the queues for goods just as long. That year a vast effort was made to get Cuba self-sufficient in rice, the people's main staple food. A bulldozer brigade cleared vast unused lands. Several varieties of top-yield rice (tested in experimental stations) were sown by eight specially designed Russian planes. Planes also sprayed insecticides and fertilized, and two high-yield crops a year resulted. Today, Cuba is self-sufficient in rice.

Shortly after the rice effort was launched, Fidel decided it was time for one gigantic leap, one huge blow which would get Cuba's economy solvent. Che was dead by then and the country was down. One more mammoth mobilization would get Cubans out of their depression, he thought, and really help Cuba in the process. The plan: to process ten million tons of sugar, almost three million more than ever before.

All of Cuba was mobilized. Fidel worked around the clock, haranguing, pleading, coaxing, stimulating —and cutting. Every Cuban revolutionary spent every free second cutting. Cabinet meetings often took place in Fidel's tent in the field. Visitors were astounded by the sight. Rows of army cots, unmade, littered with jackets, papers, pistol belts, and state papers, lined the sides. A long table covered with soda bottles, orange peel, cigar and cigarette butts served as a work desk. When it rained too hard to cut cane, Fidel and his government comrades played dominoes, joking, laughing, teasing each other. It seemed like the headquarters of an all-male hunting safari, not the seat of government. But then, that's the way Cuban revolutionaries have always been; luxuries inevitably make them uncomfortable.

No one had much time in 1969 and '70 to even think of luxuries anyway. It was sugar, from morning to night. "The honor of the Revolution is at stake," Fidel said, over and over again. By January 1970, he boasted they would do it. He had the statistics to prove it. By April, he was asking double effort—fourteen hours, sixteen hours a day. He himself was working twenty, and so was the whole government. By May, he was sad. "I'm not going to beat about the bush," he said, and Fidel has never lied, "we won't make it." On July 26, the day the harvest was to end, the Fidelista newspaper *Granma* honestly headlined: "WE HAVE FAILED."

In his speech, Fidel explained that they had harvested about 8.5 million, much more than ever before, enough to get needed foreign currencies to buy new machinery, raw materials and goods. But the real cost, he said frankly, was disastrous. The harvest had sucked away manpower, resources, and government attention from almost every other aspect of the country's economy. Hardest hit was the diversification program, that drive to make Cuba self-sufficient. Thus, shortages would continue for a long time—and so would the queues.

Fidel also explained who was to blame. Poor planning and bad organization were two reasons. Too often cut sugar stayed stacked on the field instead of being rushed to the refinery mills, and sugar canes lose their yield with each day they remain unrefined. But most crucial, said Fidel, was the stupidity of the government, "and me in particular." He offered to resign. The half million people listening unleashed a horrendous, pained "NO!" Never in their history had they had such an honest government, such a frank and truthful leader. They would stick with him no matter what.

13

But few people outside Cuba understood that the honesty with which Cubans faced their failures was a sure sign of their ultimate strength. Foreign intellectuals began to criticize the regime. In France and Italy, big-name writers and journalists who not long before had shared Fidel's tent and inner thoughts started to publish articles against him.

Then the Padilla affair broke. Herberto Padilla was a Cuban poet who wrote love poems, spent his time with foreigners, scoffed at die-hard revolutionaries, and was, as anyone who met him could testify, obnoxious both as a human being and to the Cuban Revolution. When things were going well enough, the Cuban Government ignored him. But now, after the defeat of the harvest, the hard times facing Cuba, the increase in what revolutionaries call "anti-social behavior" (loafing, drunkenness, drug addiction), the government was no longer in a mood to be tolerant. It arrested Padilla and tossed him in jail for "counterrevolutionary attitudes." A few days later, before the press and the intellectual world, Padilla publicly confessed to the charges before him.

The intellectuals of America and Europe were shocked. Some claimed Padilla had been tortured. All condemned Fidel for letting such a spectacle take place.

For most of the intellectuals, who treasure their special privileges which any revolution would take away, the Padilla affair was just an excuse to break with Fidel. They hadn't done so before because they did not want to be thought of as being on the side of the United States. Now they could do so and claim their reason was humanism. For other intellectuals, however, the Padilla affair and the fact that Cuba had supported the Russian invasion of Czechoslovakia were proof that Fidel had finally gone into the Soviet camp lock, stock, and barrel. Jean-Paul Sartre, for example, is genuinely on the side of revolution. Yet he insists that the job of the intellectual is to criticize honestly, and thus he condemned the Cuban Government for its use of "Stalinist" methods.

The Cubans did not answer. They merely concerned themselves with problems at home. They got tough. Strict anti-loafing and anti-absentee laws were passed. But more effort was put into satisfying everyday demands. More and more consumer goods were made available—at cheap prices. Coffee bars, which Cubans treasure, were opened everywhere, even in the smallest hamlets. And the last vestiges of privileges were eliminated. Padilla and the other individualistic intellectuals were given teaching jobs, usually in secondary schools, and as they discovered new meaning to life, became better human beings. They finally understood that it can never be fair for one person, just because he has a better education and has traveled more than others and can write well about his experiences, to stand apart and not do his share of the work or take on his share of the responsibilities. Besides, when the world is made up of rich and poor, the education of the rich is made possible only by the sweat of the poor. In a collective society, no man can be worth more than any other.

To build a collective society, a society of real equals, had been the goal of the Cuban revolutionaries. It was still their goal, and most Cubans continued to have faith in them. The revolutionaries had made many mistakes. No matter how great was their leader, Fidel, no matter how much faith they had in him, all revolutionaries, Fidel included, had to learn that they could not handle everything themselves. For their country to be as great as they hoped, they would have to learn to let all the people take part in making laws and setting policies. The government and the party would have to decentralize. People would have to be encouraged to question everything, in order to turn everything they agreed upon into their own achievements.

By 1973, it was becoming clear that Fidel and the leaders of the Cuban Revolution had indeed learned such lessons. Unions were encouraged to bring together their members at the local level to discuss policy, analyze problems, and offer solutions. Community decision-making was being institutionalized. Each citizen, worker or peasant, educated or not, was now sure that he mattered and that his voice, in the collective, was being heard.

Today, Cuban leaders are still obsessed primarily with building up their country. They want to eliminate five centuries of misery in just a few years. In their zeal, it is unfortunately natural that they make mistakes. But it must never be forgotten that in barely a dozen years, they have given most Cubans hope and dignity, and taught each other and most of the island's seven million people to trust each other. That's already a whole new world.

Index

and Moncada Barracks assault, 28–39; orders first attack from Sierra Maestra on lowlands, 67–70; organizes action cells after Batista's takeover, 28; and Padilla affair, 129–31; as Prime Minister, 86ff.; on reactionaries, revolutionaries and the people, 117; reforms, problems, and progress, 91–93, 94ff., 122–28, 129–32; and revolutions outside Cuba, 114–15, 119–21; sensitivity to injustices in, 1–2 15–27 *passim;* simplicity of manner and style, 97–98; and Soviet Union (see *under* Soviet Union); speaking ability of, 19, 31–38, 98; as student revolutionary, 14–25; takes control following Batista's downfall, 84ff.; trial and imprisonment of, 31–39, 40–41; and trials of war criminals, 86–91; and 26th of July Movement (see 26th of July Movement)
Castro, Fidelito (son), 25, 84
Castro, Juanna (sister), 15
Castro, Lina Ruz (mother), 15, 16, 95
Castro, Ramón (brother), 15–16, 95
Castro, Raúl (brother), 15, 16, 17, 44, 69, 70, 71, 74, 84, 85–86, 99, 116; and *Granma* expedition, 52, 56; and Moncada Barracks assault, 30, 32, 39
Chao, and *Granma* expedition, 51, 55
Chibas, Eduardo, 26–27, 41, 42
Chibas, Raúl, 41
Chile, 121
China, 110, 121, 125
Chomón, Fauré, 66, 78, 81
CIA, 43, 88, 100, 102, 104, 120
Cienfuegos, Camilo, 53, 55, 78, 79–80, 81, 82
Colombia, 23–25, 114
Communism (Communists), 21, 98–99, 100, 101, 106, 111–12, 116–17. See also specific countries, parties
Communist Party (of Cuba), 21, 57, 116–17; Central Committee, 116–17; Political Bureau, 116–17

Congo, 114, 115, 118, 119
Corinthia expedition, 69–70
Crespo, Abelardo, 37
Cuba: Batista's seizure of power with Army (1952), 27, 28ff.; Castro and (see Castro, Fidel); Cuban Revolution and, 28–39, 40–48, 49–64, 65–77, 78–83 (see also Cuban Revolution; specific aspects, individuals); hurricane (October 1963), 126; and independence, 5–10; map of, ii; pre-Revolution, 1–14; progress, reforms, and problems under Castro, 91–93, 94ff., 122–28, 129–32; Spain and, 4–7; United States and, 4–11 (see also United States of America)
Cuban Revolution, 28–39, 40–48, 49–64, 65–77, 78–83, 84ff. (see also specific aspects, events, individuals, organizations); Castro and (see Castro, Fidel); *Granma* expedition and, 45–48, 49–64, 65ff.; and reforms, progress and problems after success of, 91–93, 94ff., 122–28, 129–32; Soviet Union and (see Soviet Union); and trials of war criminals, 84–93; United States and, 60, 62, 84–91, 93, 96, 98–104, 105–13, 114–15, 118–19, 120
Czechoslovakia, 119, 130

Del Pino, Rafael, 23, 25
Díaz Balart, Mirtha (wife), 25, 41
Díaz Tamayo, General Martín, 36
Dominican Republic, 21–22, 23
Dorticós Torrado, O., 99, 126

Echevarría, José Antonio, 66, 77
Economy, 91, 92–93, 94–96 (see also Agriculture; Land); Cuban Revolution and progress and problems in, 122–28, 131–32; diversification program, 125, 128
Education (schools), 2, 9, 75, 91, 92, 95, 122, 131
Eisenhower, Dwight, 64, 93, 101–2
Ellender, Allen J., 82
El Uvero, attack on, 70

JOHN GERASSI is the author of numerous books on Latin America, former Latin-American editor for *Time, Newsweek, Ramparts* magazines and New York *Times* correspondent in Latin America. He has taught Political Science at the New School for Social Research, Journalism at New York University, International Relations at San Francisco State College. He has visited Cuba on many occasions and knows Fidel Castro personally.